STAR WARS®

KNIGHTS OF THE OLD REPUBLIC

VOLUME NINE
DEMON

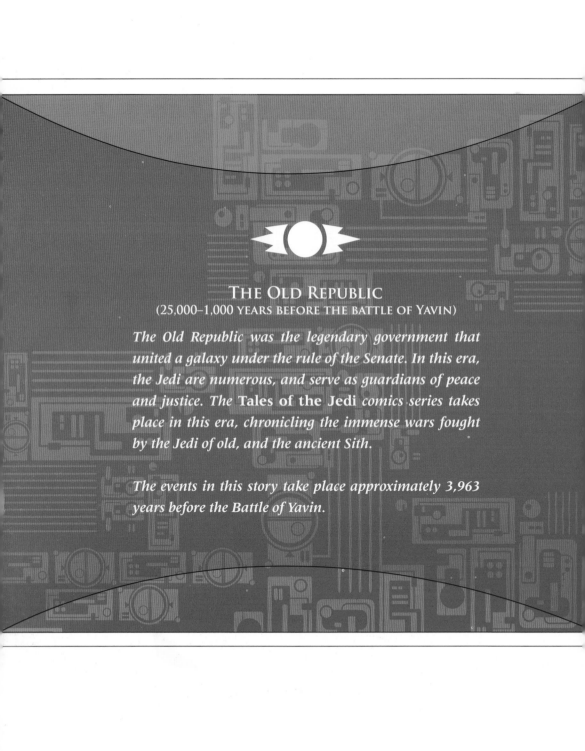

THE OLD REPUBLIC
(25,000–1,000 YEARS BEFORE THE BATTLE OF YAVIN)

*The Old Republic was the legendary government that united a galaxy under the rule of the Senate. In this era, the Jedi are numerous, and serve as guardians of peace and justice. The **Tales of the Jedi** comics series takes place in this era, chronicling the immense wars fought by the Jedi of old, and the ancient Sith.*

The events in this story take place approximately 3,963 years before the Battle of Yavin.

STAR WARS®

KNIGHTS OF THE OLD REPUBLIC

VOLUME NINE
DEMON

SCRIPT JOHN JACKSON MILLER

ART BRIAN CHING

COLORS MICHAEL ATIYEH

LETTERING MICHAEL HEISLER

FRONT & BACK COVER ART BENJAMIN CARRÉ

Dark Horse Books®

PUBLISHER MIKE RICHARDSON

ASSISTANT EDITOR FREDDYE LINS

EDITOR DAVE MARSHALL

Special thanks to Jann Moorhead, David Anderman, Troy Alders, Leland Chee,
Sue Rostoni, and Carol Roeder at Lucas Licensing.

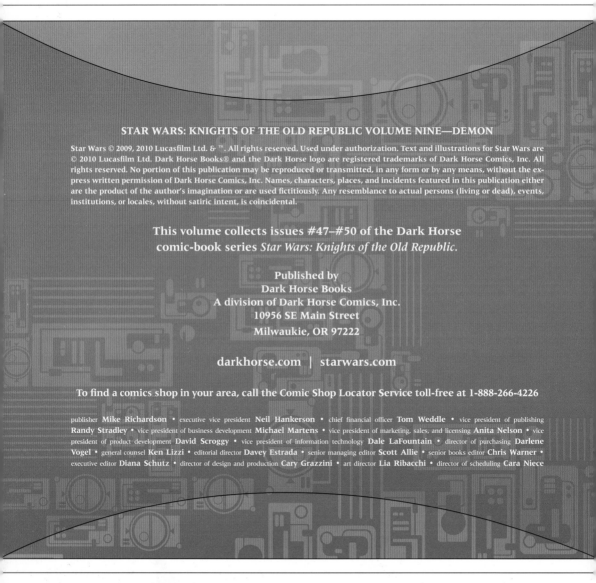

STAR WARS: KNIGHTS OF THE OLD REPUBLIC VOLUME NINE—DEMON

This volume collects issues #47–#50 of the Dark Horse
comic-book series Star Wars: Knights of the Old Republic.

Published by
Dark Horse Books
A division of Dark Horse Comics, Inc.
10956 SE Main Street
Milwaukie, OR 97222

darkhorse.com | starwars.com

To find a comics shop in your area, call the Comic Shop Locator Service toll-free at 1-888-266-4226

publisher Mike Richardson • executive vice president Neil Hankerson • chief financial officer Tom Weddle • vice president of publishing Randy Stradley • vice president of business development Michael Martens • vice president of marketing, sales, and licensing Anita Nelson • vice president of product development David Scroggy • vice president of information technology Dale LaFountain • director of purchasing Darlene Vogel • general counsel Ken Lizzi • editorial director Davey Estrada • senior managing editor Scott Allie • senior books editor Chris Warner • executive editor Diana Schutz • director of design and production Cary Grazzini • art director Lia Ribacchi • director of scheduling Cara Niece

First edition: July 2010
ISBN 978-1-59582-476-9

1 3 5 7 9 10 8 6 4 2
Printed at Midas Printing International, Ltd., Huizhou, China

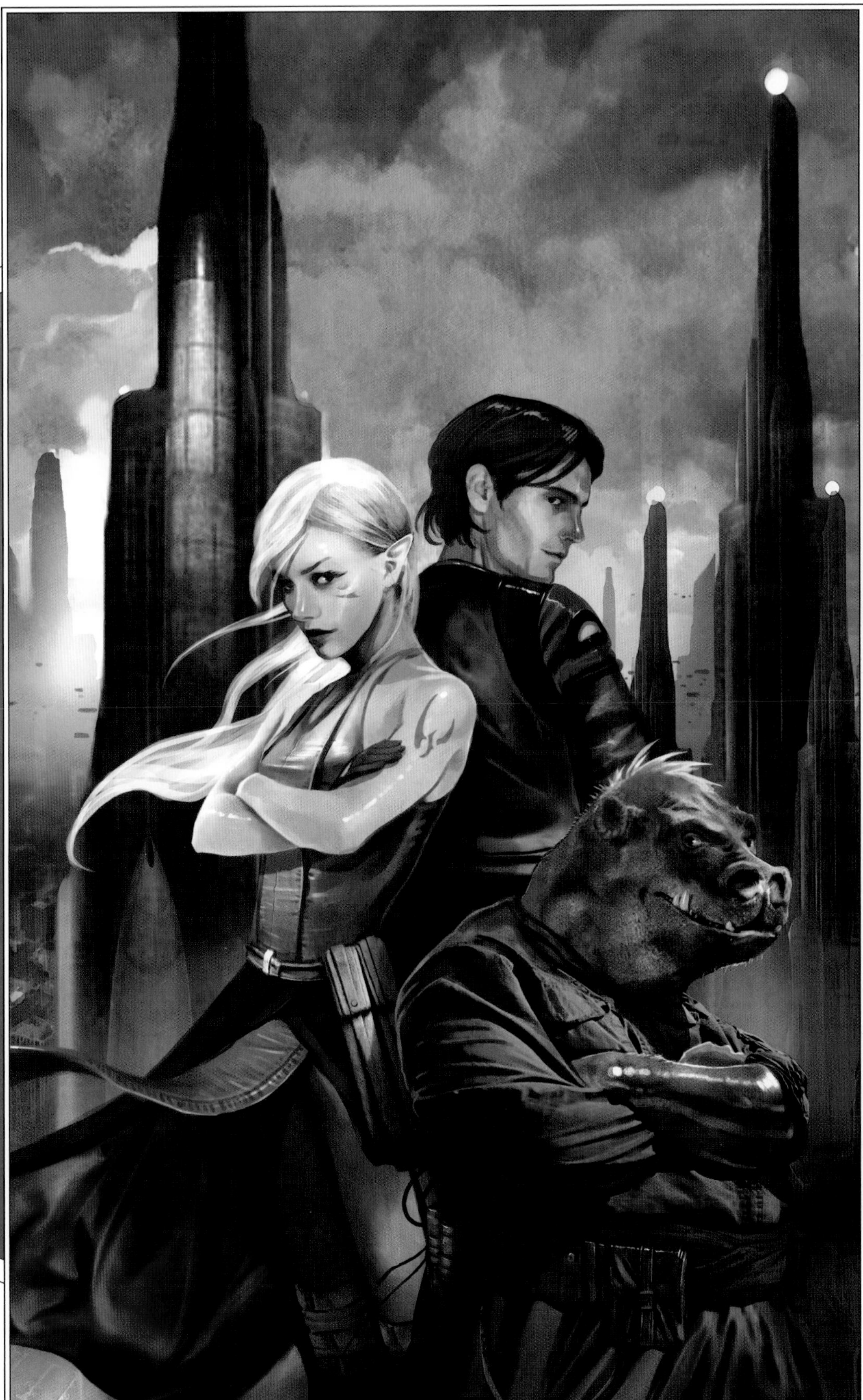

ILLUSTRATION BY BENJAMIN CARRÉ

DEMON

Months earlier, former Padawan Zayne Carrick helped capture Demagol, the twisted Mandalorian biologist. Now, with Demagol awakened from his coma, Zayne and his con-artist partner Gryph are called to the Republic capital to testify in the show trial of the age.

The call comes just as Zayne parts with another Mandalorian, the enigmatic Rohlan, and with Jarael, his fierce warrior ally. His faith in her shaken by his encounter with Chantique—the vindictive, Force-using leader of the Crucible slaver organization— Zayne has driven Jarael away.

His team splintered, Zayne's adventures finally seem at an end. But Zayne's fortunes, as ever, are poised for another turn. Surprises—and dangers—await in quarters where he never suspected them . . .

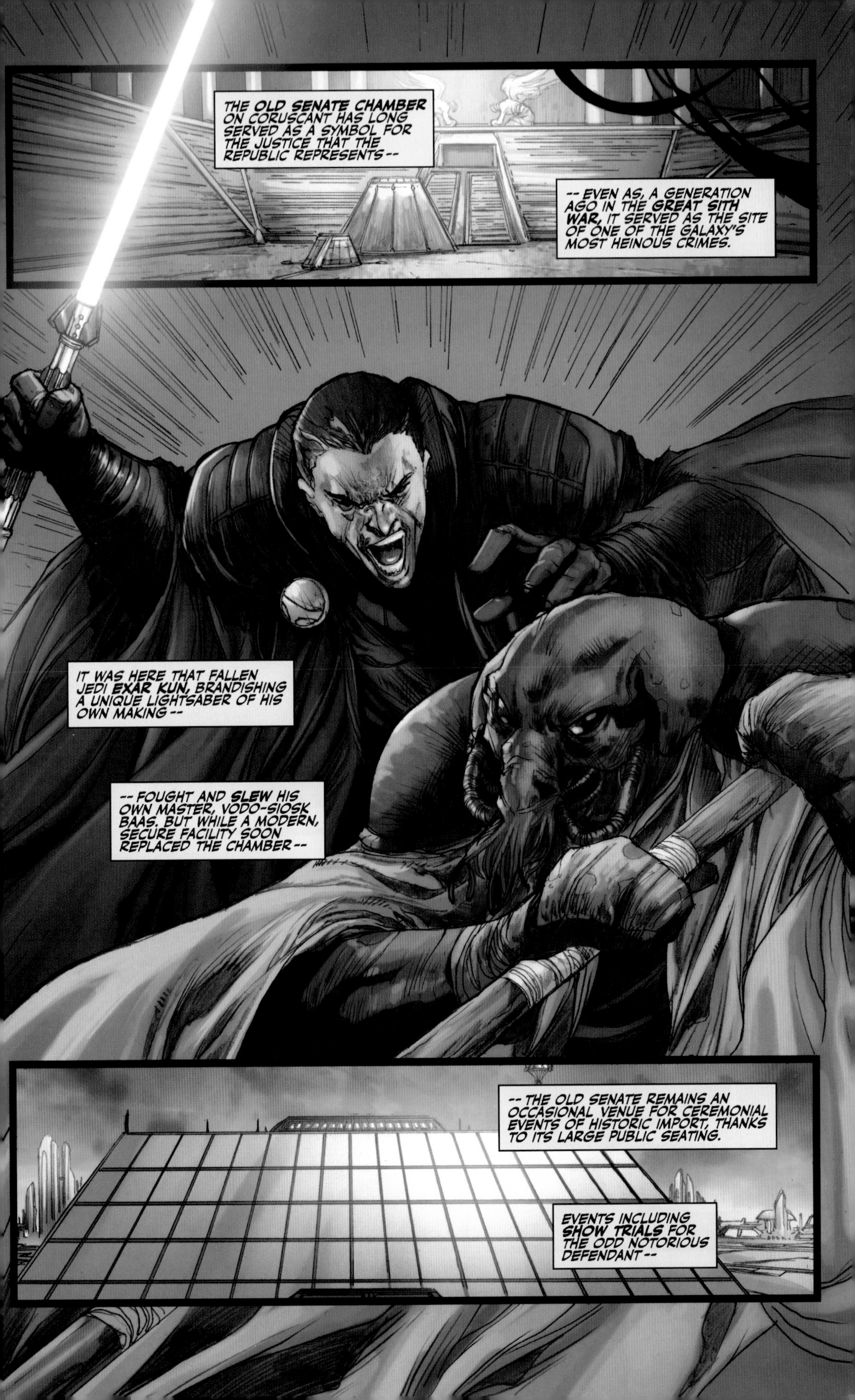
THE OLD SENATE CHAMBER ON CORUSCANT HAS LONG SERVED AS A SYMBOL FOR THE JUSTICE THAT THE REPUBLIC REPRESENTS--
--EVEN AS, A GENERATION AGO IN THE GREAT SITH WAR, IT SERVED AS THE SITE OF ONE OF THE GALAXY'S MOST HEINOUS CRIMES.
IT WAS HERE THAT FALLEN JEDI EXAR KUN, BRANDISHING A UNIQUE LIGHTSABER OF HIS OWN MAKING--
--FOUGHT AND SLEW HIS OWN MASTER, VODO-SIOSK BAAS. BUT WHILE A MODERN, SECURE FACILITY SOON REPLACED THE CHAMBER--
--THE OLD SENATE REMAINS AN OCCASIONAL VENUE FOR CEREMONIAL EVENTS OF HISTORIC IMPORT, THANKS TO ITS LARGE PUBLIC SEATING.
EVENTS INCLUDING SHOW TRIALS FOR THE ODD NOTORIOUS DEFENDANT--

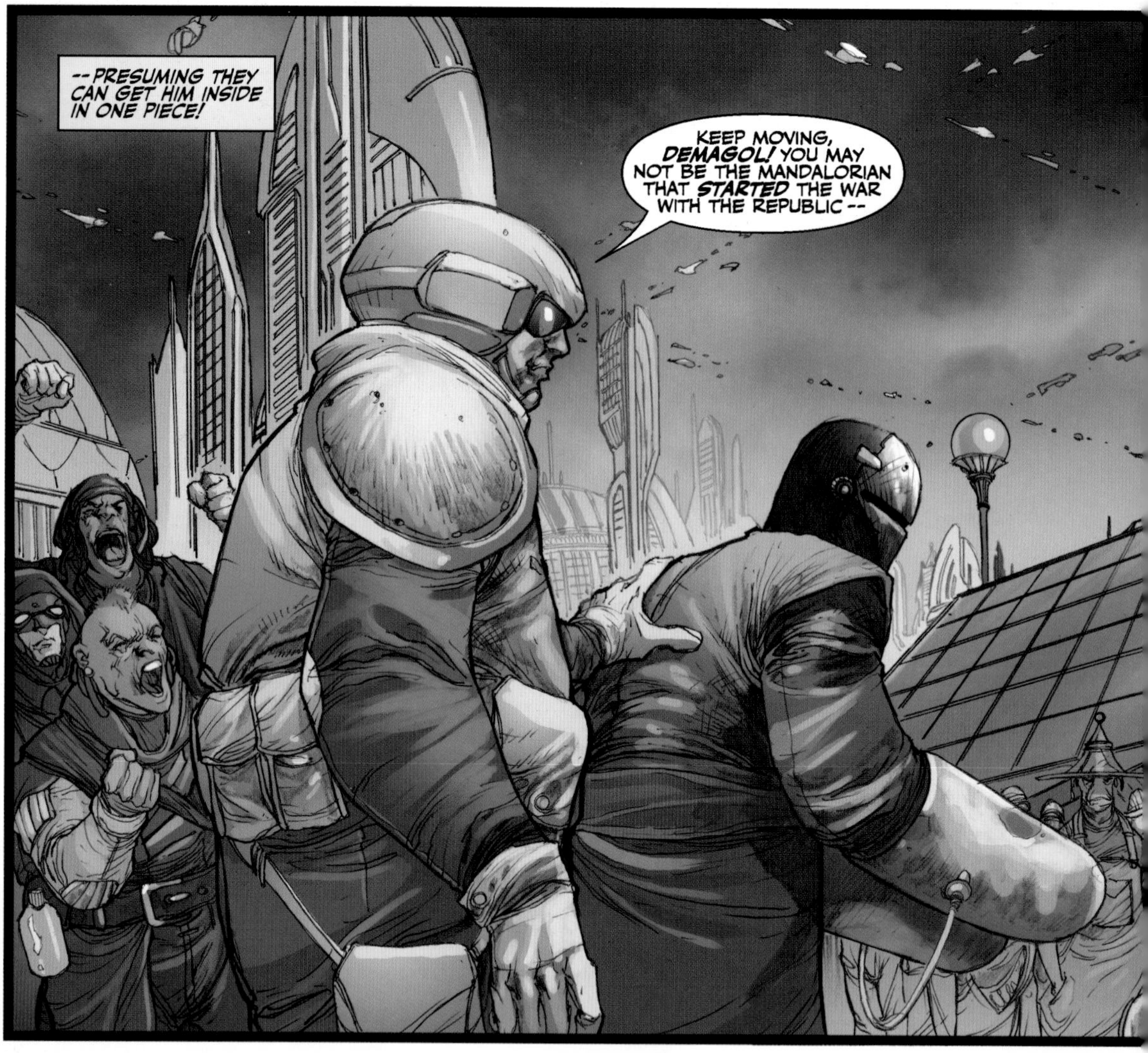
--PRESUMING THEY CAN GET HIM INSIDE IN ONE PIECE!
KEEP MOVING, DEMAGOL! YOU MAY NOT BE THE MANDALORIAN THAT STARTED THE WAR WITH THE REPUBLIC--

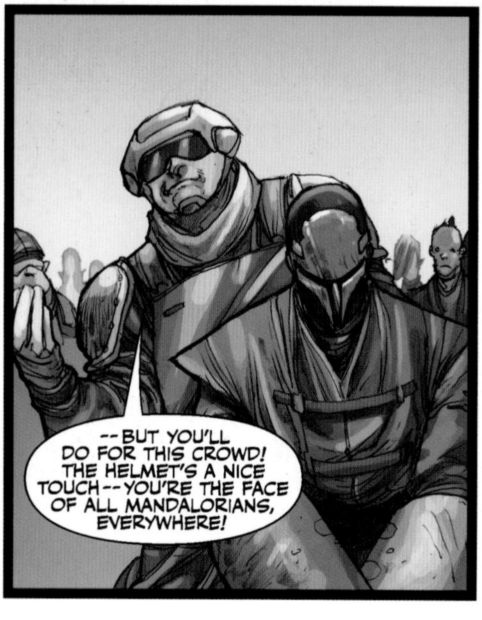
--BUT YOU'LL DO FOR THIS CROWD! THE HELMET'S A NICE TOUCH--YOU'RE THE FACE OF ALL MANDALORIANS, EVERYWHERE!

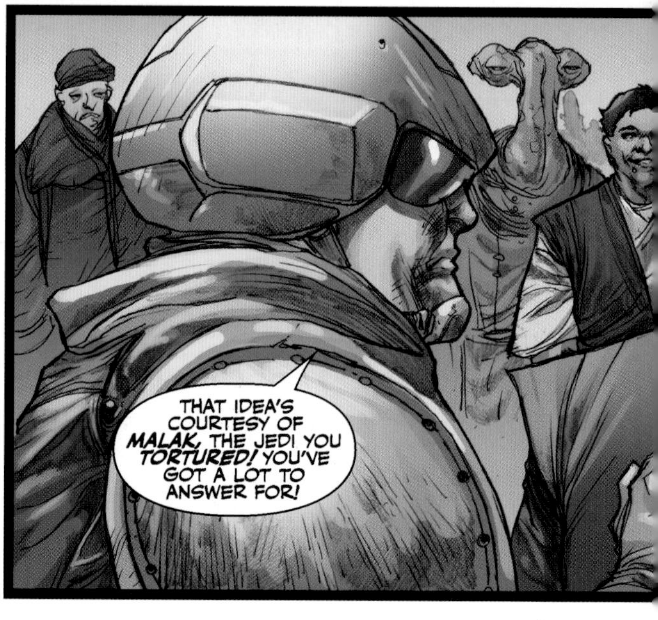
THAT IDEA'S COURTESY OF MALAK, THE JEDI YOU TORTURED! YOU'VE GOT A LOT TO ANSWER FOR!

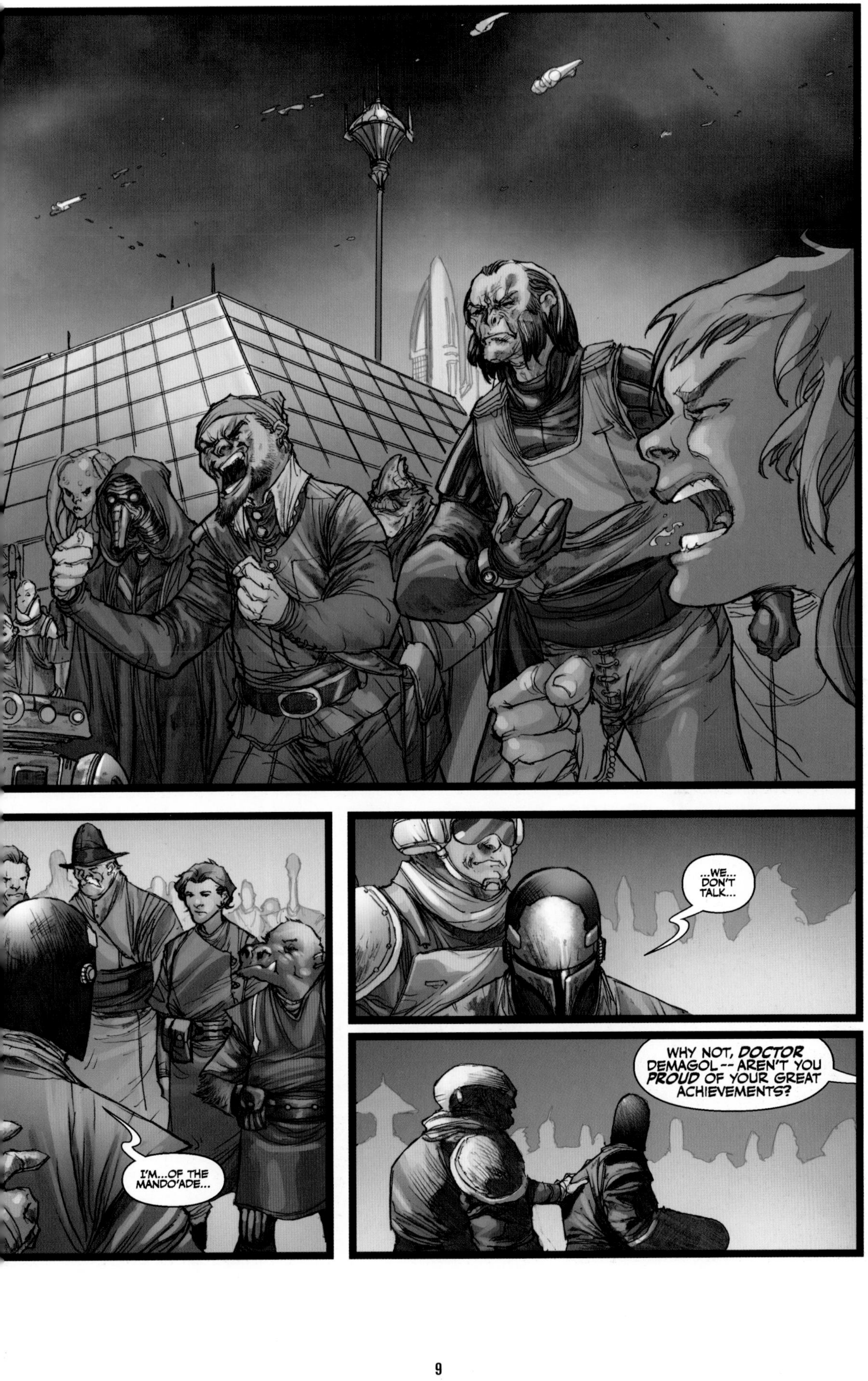
I'M...OF THE MANDO'ADE...
...WE... DON'T TALK...
WHY NOT, *DOCTOR* DEMAGOL-- AREN'T YOU *PROUD* OF YOUR GREAT ACHIEVEMENTS?

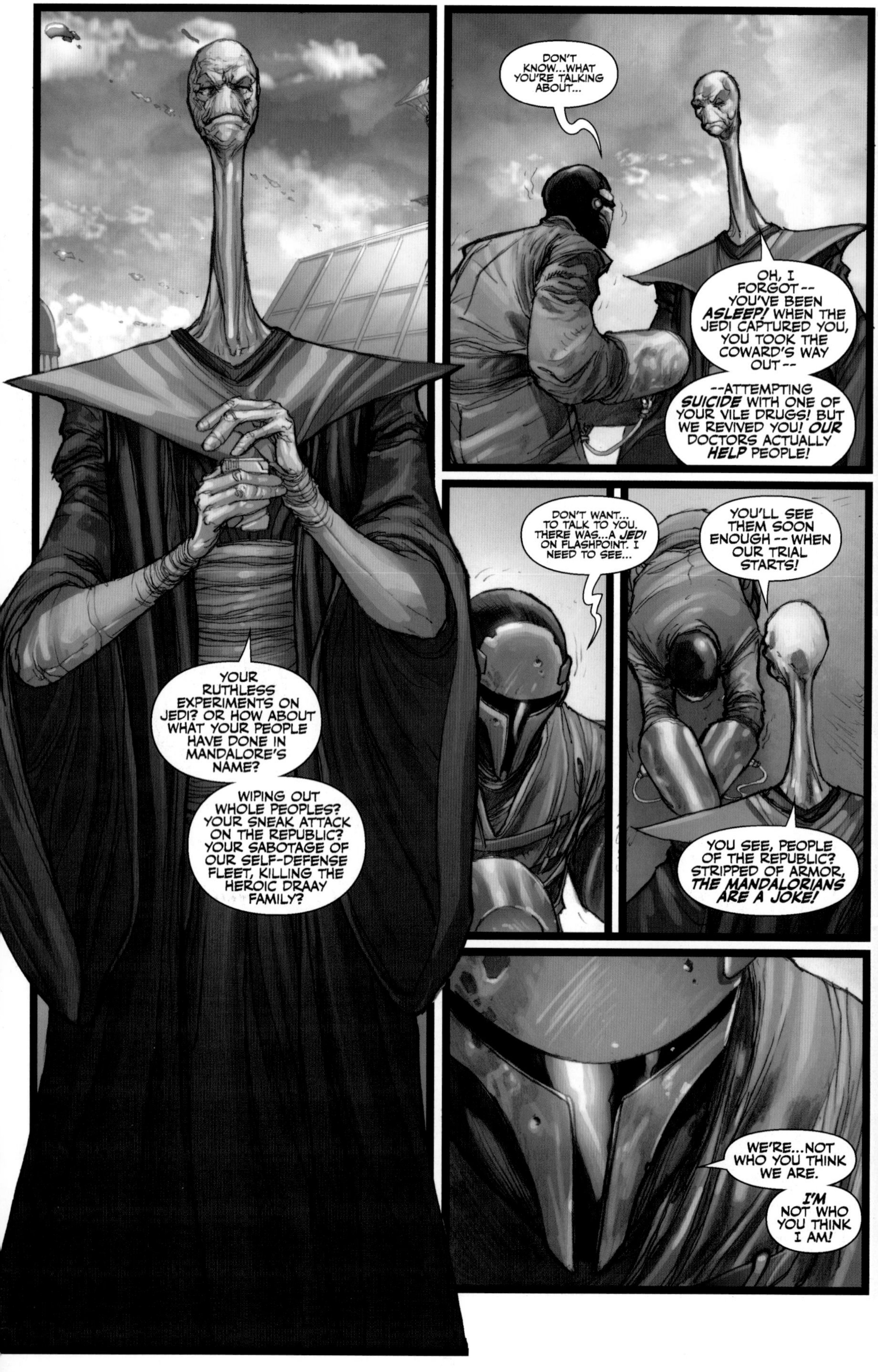
YOUR RUTHLESS EXPERIMENTS ON JEDI? OR HOW ABOUT WHAT YOUR PEOPLE HAVE DONE IN MANDALORE'S NAME?
WIPING OUT WHOLE PEOPLES? YOUR SNEAK ATTACK ON THE REPUBLIC? YOUR SABOTAGE OF OUR SELF-DEFENSE FLEET, KILLING THE HEROIC DRAAY FAMILY?
DON'T KNOW...WHAT YOU'RE TALKING ABOUT...
OH, I FORGOT-- YOU'VE BEEN *ASLEEP!* WHEN THE JEDI CAPTURED YOU, YOU TOOK THE COWARD'S WAY OUT--
--ATTEMPTING *SUICIDE* WITH ONE OF YOUR VILE DRUGS! BUT WE REVIVED YOU! *OUR* DOCTORS ACTUALLY *HELP* PEOPLE!
DON'T WANT... TO TALK TO YOU. THERE WAS...A *JEDI* ON FLASHPOINT. I NEED TO SEE...
YOU'LL SEE THEM SOON ENOUGH -- WHEN OUR TRIAL STARTS!
YOU SEE, PEOPLE OF THE REPUBLIC? STRIPPED OF ARMOR, *THE MANDALORIANS ARE A JOKE!*
WE'RE...NOT WHO YOU THINK WE ARE.
I'M NOT WHO YOU THINK I AM!

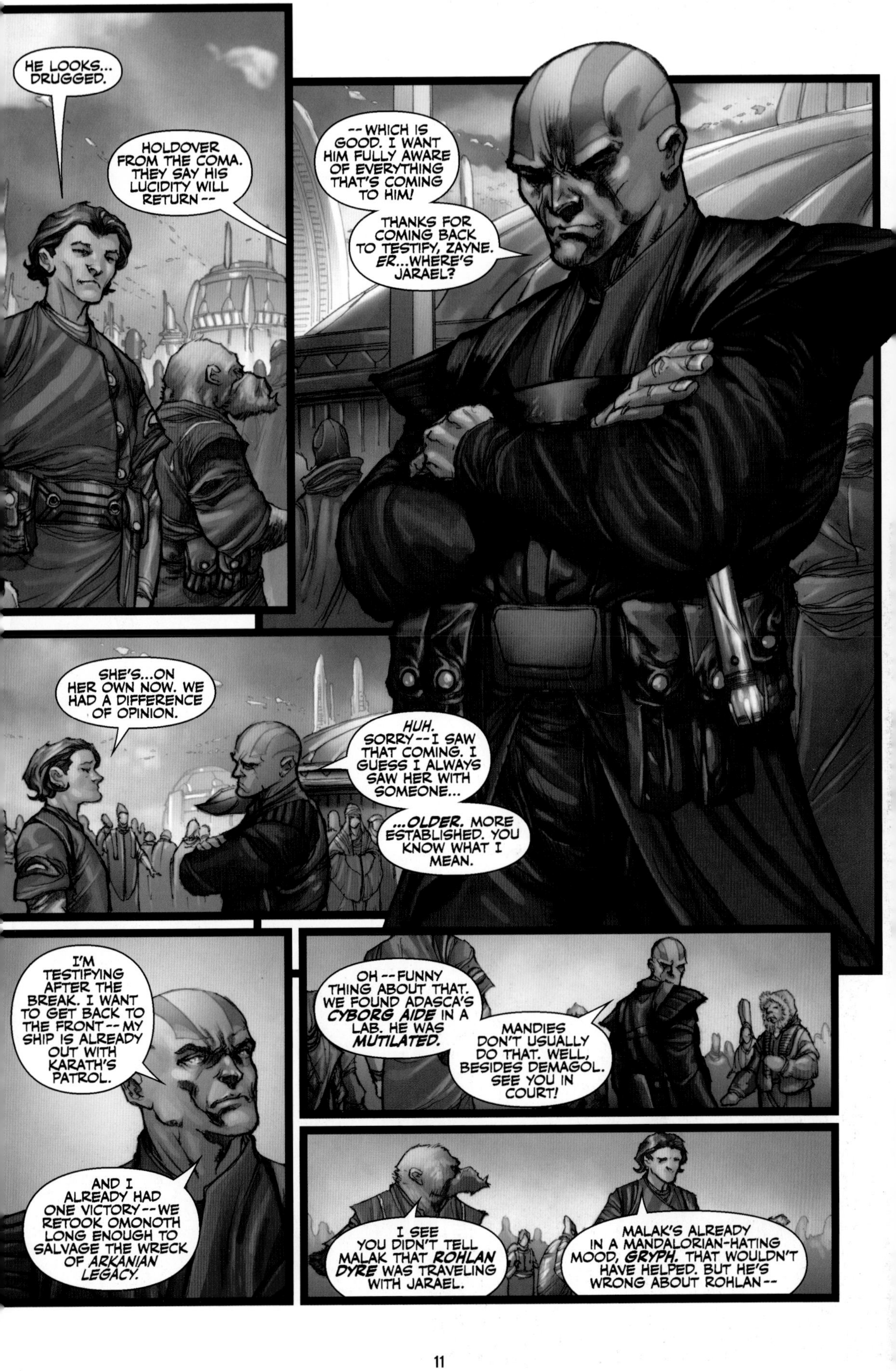
HE LOOKS... DRUGGED.
HOLDOVER FROM THE COMA. THEY SAY HIS LUCIDITY WILL RETURN--
--WHICH IS GOOD. I WANT HIM FULLY AWARE OF EVERYTHING THAT'S COMING TO HIM!
THANKS FOR COMING BACK TO TESTIFY, ZAYNE. ER...WHERE'S JARAEL?
SHE'S...ON HER OWN NOW. WE HAD A DIFFERENCE OF OPINION.
HUH. SORRY--I SAW THAT COMING. I GUESS I ALWAYS SAW HER WITH SOMEONE...
...OLDER. MORE ESTABLISHED. YOU KNOW WHAT I MEAN.
I'M TESTIFYING AFTER THE BREAK. I WANT TO GET BACK TO THE FRONT--MY SHIP IS ALREADY OUT WITH KARATH'S PATROL.
AND I ALREADY HAD ONE VICTORY--WE RETOOK OMONOTH LONG ENOUGH TO SALVAGE THE WRECK OF ARKANIAN LEGACY.
OH--FUNNY THING ABOUT THAT. WE FOUND ADASCA'S CYBORG AIDE IN A LAB. HE WAS MUTILATED.
MANDIES DON'T USUALLY DO THAT. WELL, BESIDES DEMAGOL. SEE YOU IN COURT!
I SEE YOU DIDN'T TELL MALAK THAT ROHLAN DYRE WAS TRAVELING WITH JARAEL.
MALAK'S ALREADY IN A MANDALORIAN-HATING MOOD, GRYPH. THAT WOULDN'T HAVE HELPED. BUT HE'S WRONG ABOUT ROHLAN--

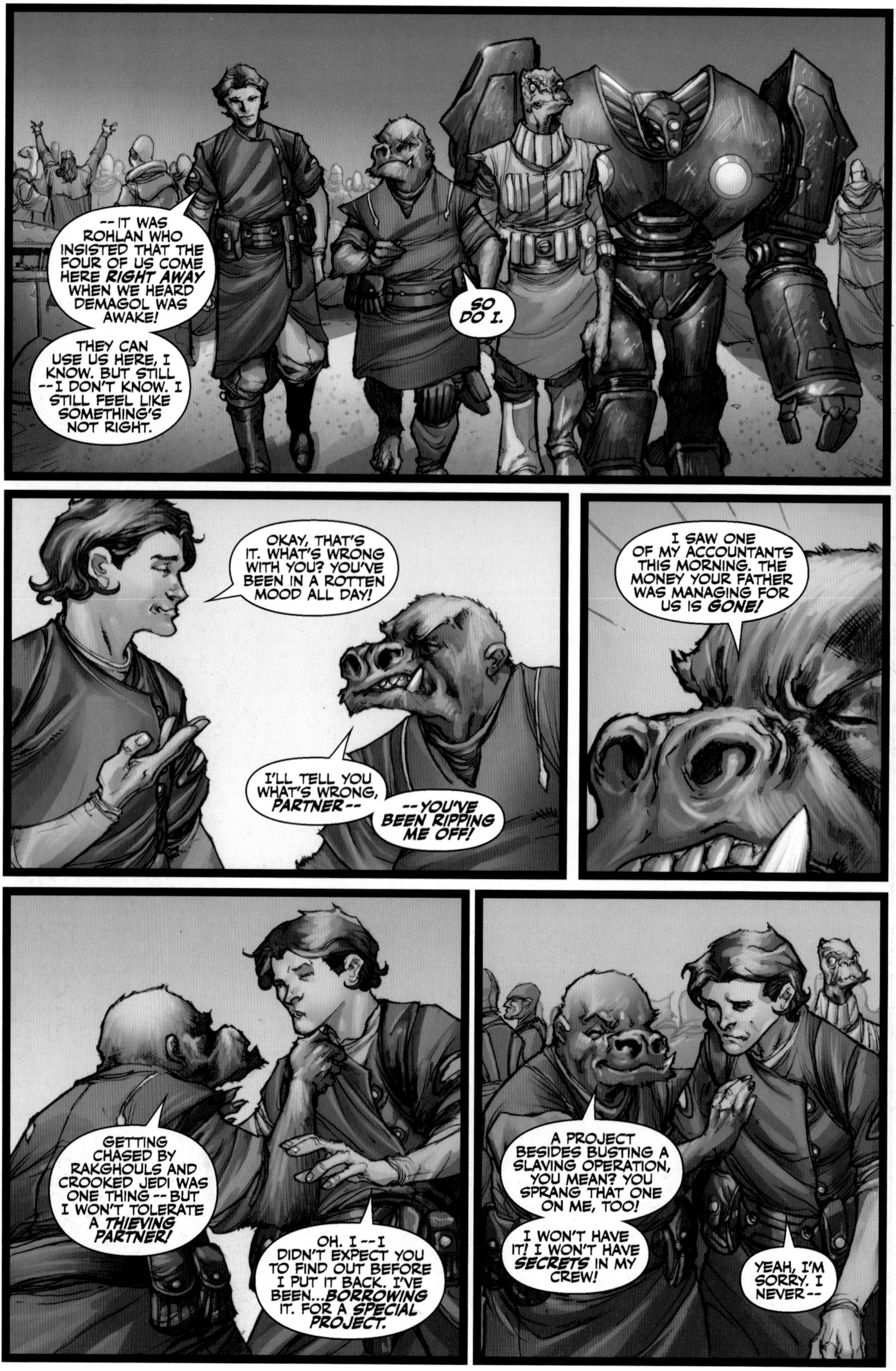
--IT WAS ROHLAN WHO INSISTED THAT THE FOUR OF US COME HERE *RIGHT AWAY* WHEN WE HEARD DEMAGOL WAS AWAKE!
THEY CAN USE US HERE, I KNOW. BUT STILL --I DON'T KNOW. I STILL FEEL LIKE SOMETHING'S NOT RIGHT.
SO DO I.
OKAY, THAT'S IT. WHAT'S WRONG WITH YOU? YOU'VE BEEN IN A ROTTEN MOOD ALL DAY!
I'LL TELL YOU WHAT'S WRONG, *PARTNER*--
--YOU'VE BEEN RIPPING ME OFF!
I SAW ONE OF MY ACCOUNTANTS THIS MORNING. THE MONEY YOUR FATHER WAS MANAGING FOR US IS *GONE!*
GETTING CHASED BY RAKGHOULS AND CROOKED JEDI WAS ONE THING--BUT I WON'T TOLERATE A *THIEVING PARTNER!*
OH. I--I DIDN'T EXPECT YOU TO FIND OUT BEFORE I PUT IT BACK. I'VE BEEN...*BORROWING* IT. FOR A *SPECIAL PROJECT.*
A PROJECT BESIDES BUSTING A SLAVING OPERATION, YOU MEAN? YOU SPRANG THAT ONE ON ME, TOO!
I WON'T HAVE IT! I WON'T HAVE *SECRETS* IN MY CREW!
YEAH, I'M SORRY. I NEVER--

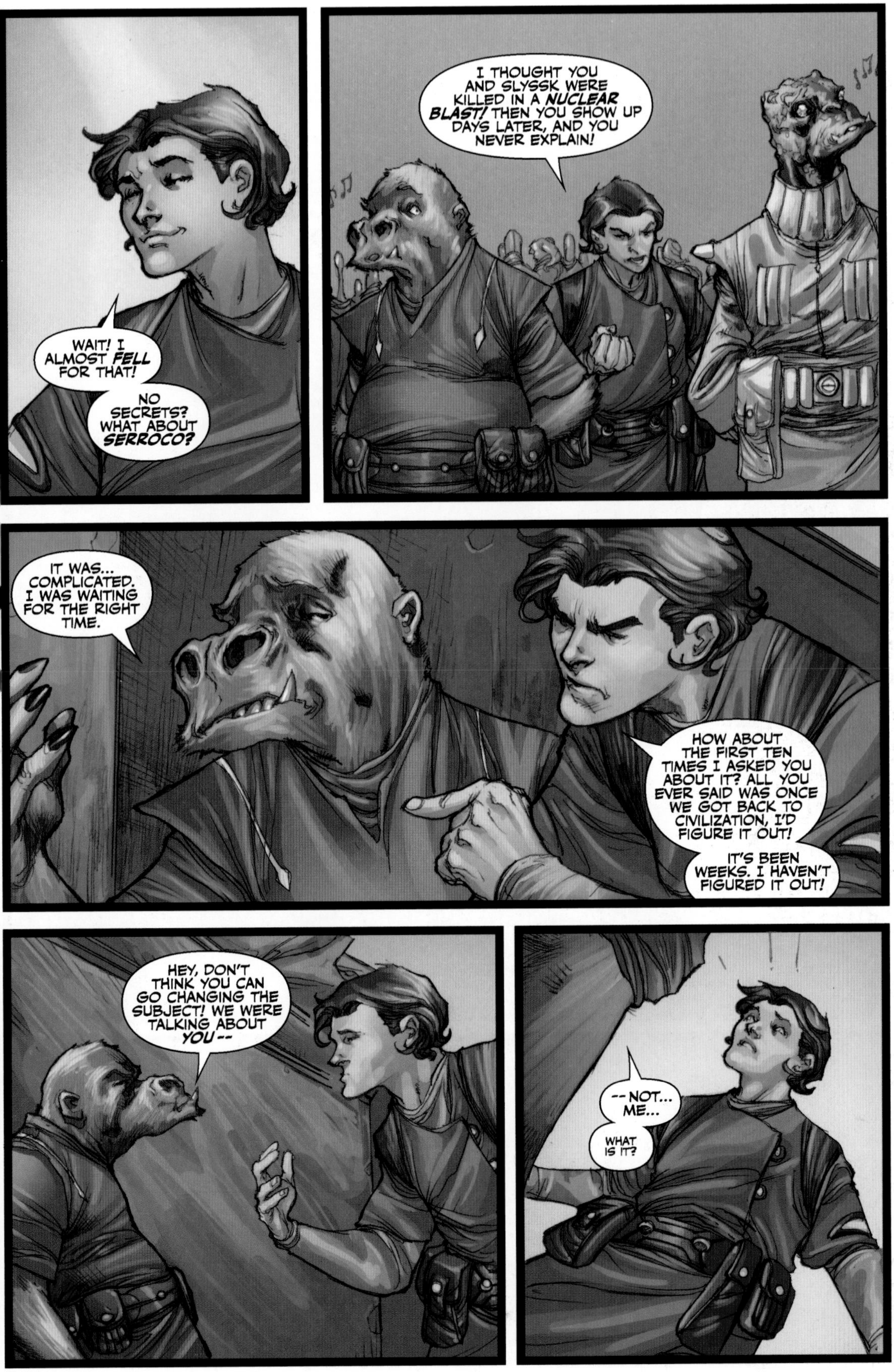
WAIT! I ALMOST FELL FOR THAT!
NO SECRETS? WHAT ABOUT SERROCO?
I THOUGHT YOU AND SLYSSK WERE KILLED IN A NUCLEAR BLAST! THEN YOU SHOW UP DAYS LATER, AND YOU NEVER EXPLAIN!
IT WAS... COMPLICATED. I WAS WAITING FOR THE RIGHT TIME.
HOW ABOUT THE FIRST TEN TIMES I ASKED YOU ABOUT IT? ALL YOU EVER SAID WAS ONCE WE GOT BACK TO CIVILIZATION, I'D FIGURE IT OUT!
IT'S BEEN WEEKS. I HAVEN'T FIGURED IT OUT!
HEY, DON'T THINK YOU CAN GO CHANGING THE SUBJECT! WE WERE TALKING ABOUT YOU--
--NOT... ME...
WHAT IS IT?

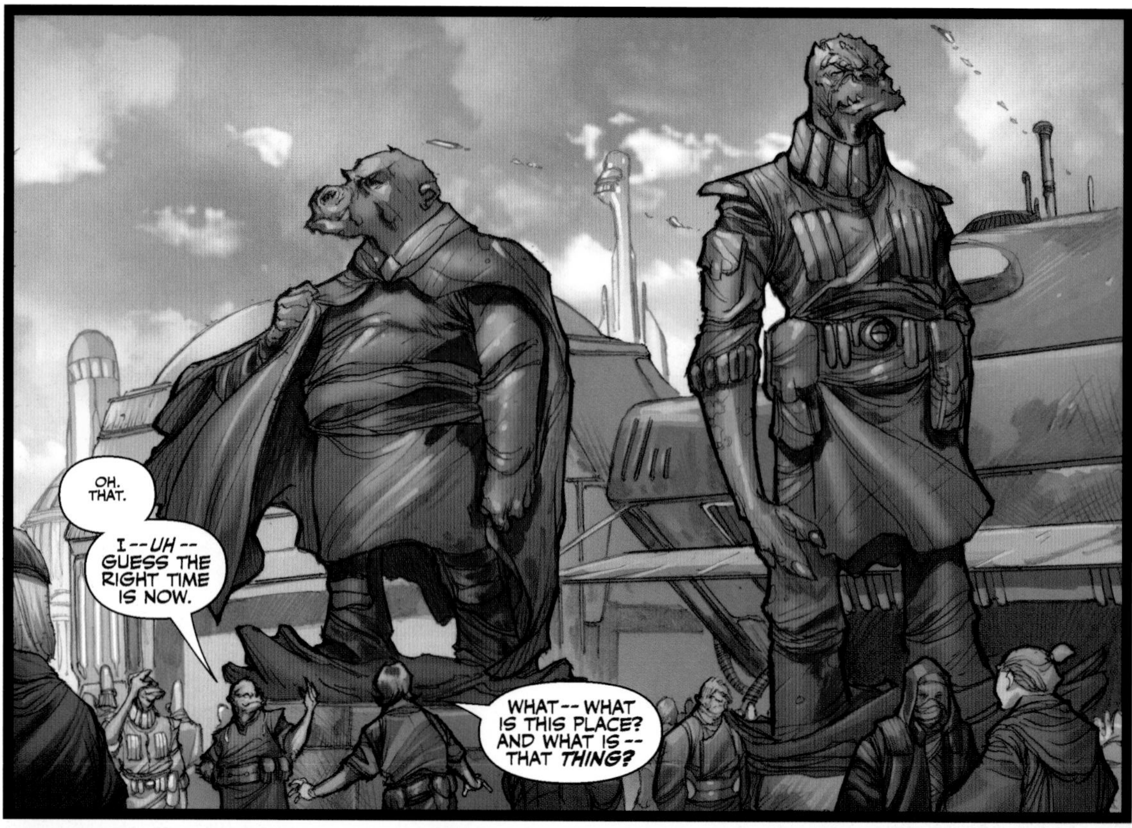
OH. THAT.
I--*UH*--GUESS THE RIGHT TIME IS NOW.
WHAT--WHAT IS THIS PLACE? AND WHAT IS--THAT *THING?*

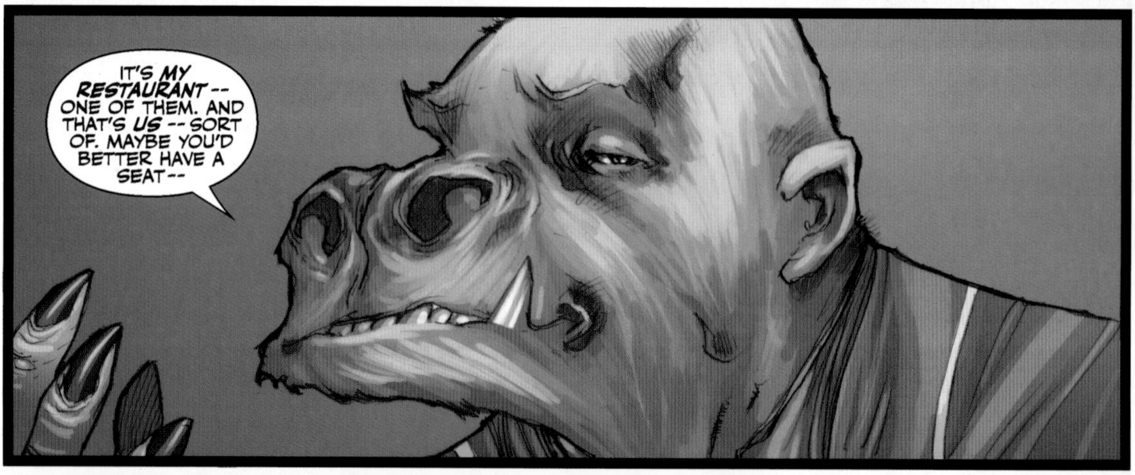
IT'S *MY RESTAURANT*--ONE OF THEM. AND THAT'S *US*--SORT OF. MAYBE YOU'D BETTER HAVE A SEAT--

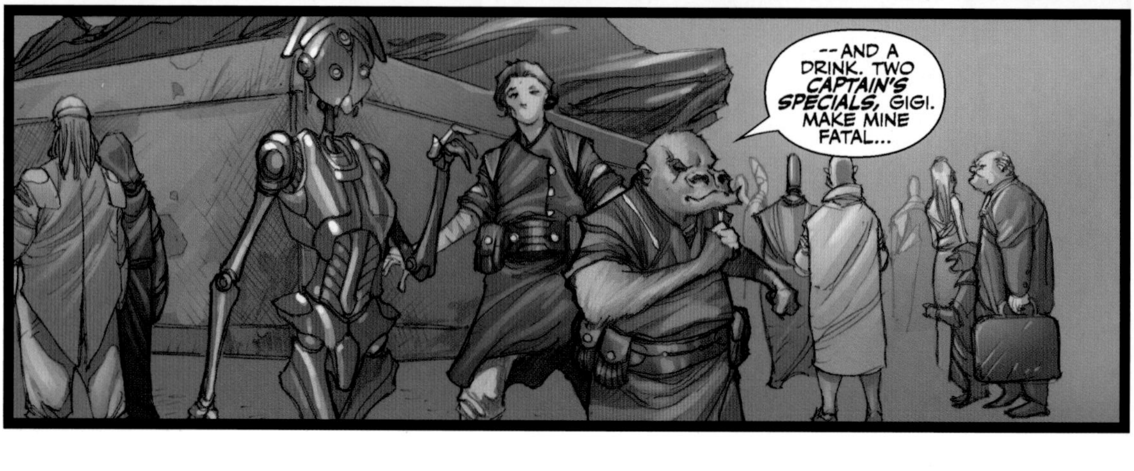
--AND A DRINK. TWO *CAPTAIN'S SPECIALS,* GIGI. MAKE MINE FATAL...

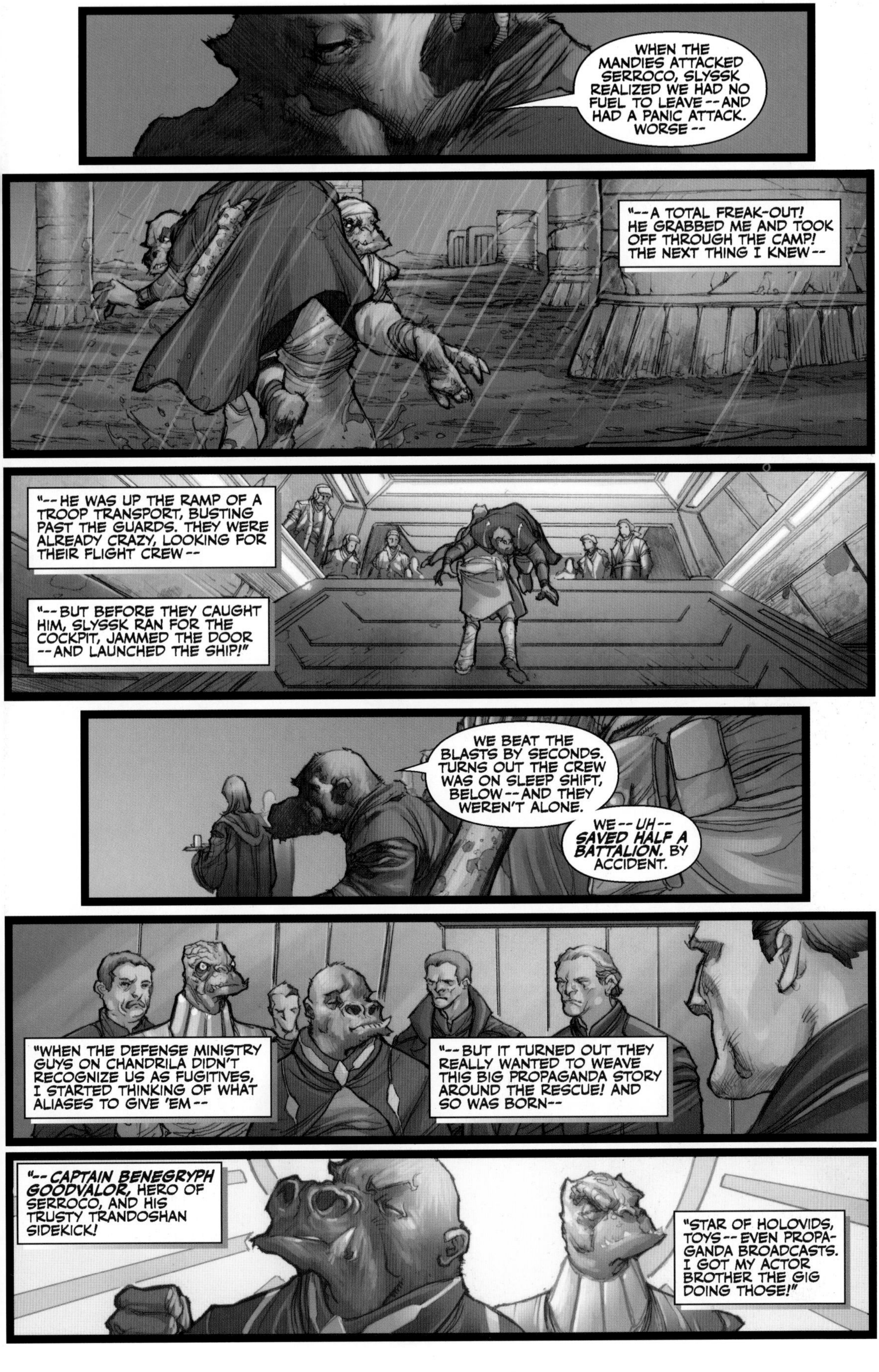
WHEN THE MANDIES ATTACKED SERROCO, SLYSSK REALIZED WE HAD NO FUEL TO LEAVE--AND HAD A PANIC ATTACK. WORSE--
"--A TOTAL FREAK-OUT! HE GRABBED ME AND TOOK OFF THROUGH THE CAMP! THE NEXT THING I KNEW--
"--HE WAS UP THE RAMP OF A TROOP TRANSPORT, BUSTING PAST THE GUARDS. THEY WERE ALREADY CRAZY, LOOKING FOR THEIR FLIGHT CREW--
"--BUT BEFORE THEY CAUGHT HIM, SLYSSK RAN FOR THE COCKPIT, JAMMED THE DOOR --AND LAUNCHED THE SHIP!"
WE BEAT THE BLASTS BY SECONDS. TURNS OUT THE CREW WAS ON SLEEP SHIFT, BELOW--AND THEY WEREN'T ALONE.
WE--*UH*-- ***SAVED HALF A BATTALION.*** BY ACCIDENT.
"WHEN THE DEFENSE MINISTRY GUYS ON CHANDRILA DIDN'T RECOGNIZE US AS FUGITIVES, I STARTED THINKING OF WHAT ALIASES TO GIVE 'EM--
"--BUT IT TURNED OUT THEY REALLY WANTED TO WEAVE THIS BIG PROPAGANDA STORY AROUND THE RESCUE! AND SO WAS BORN--
"-- ***CAPTAIN BENEGRYPH GOODVALOR,*** HERO OF SERROCO, AND HIS TRUSTY TRANDOSHAN SIDEKICK!
"STAR OF HOLOVIDS, TOYS--EVEN PROPA-GANDA BROADCASTS. I GOT MY ACTOR BROTHER THE GIG DOING THOSE!"

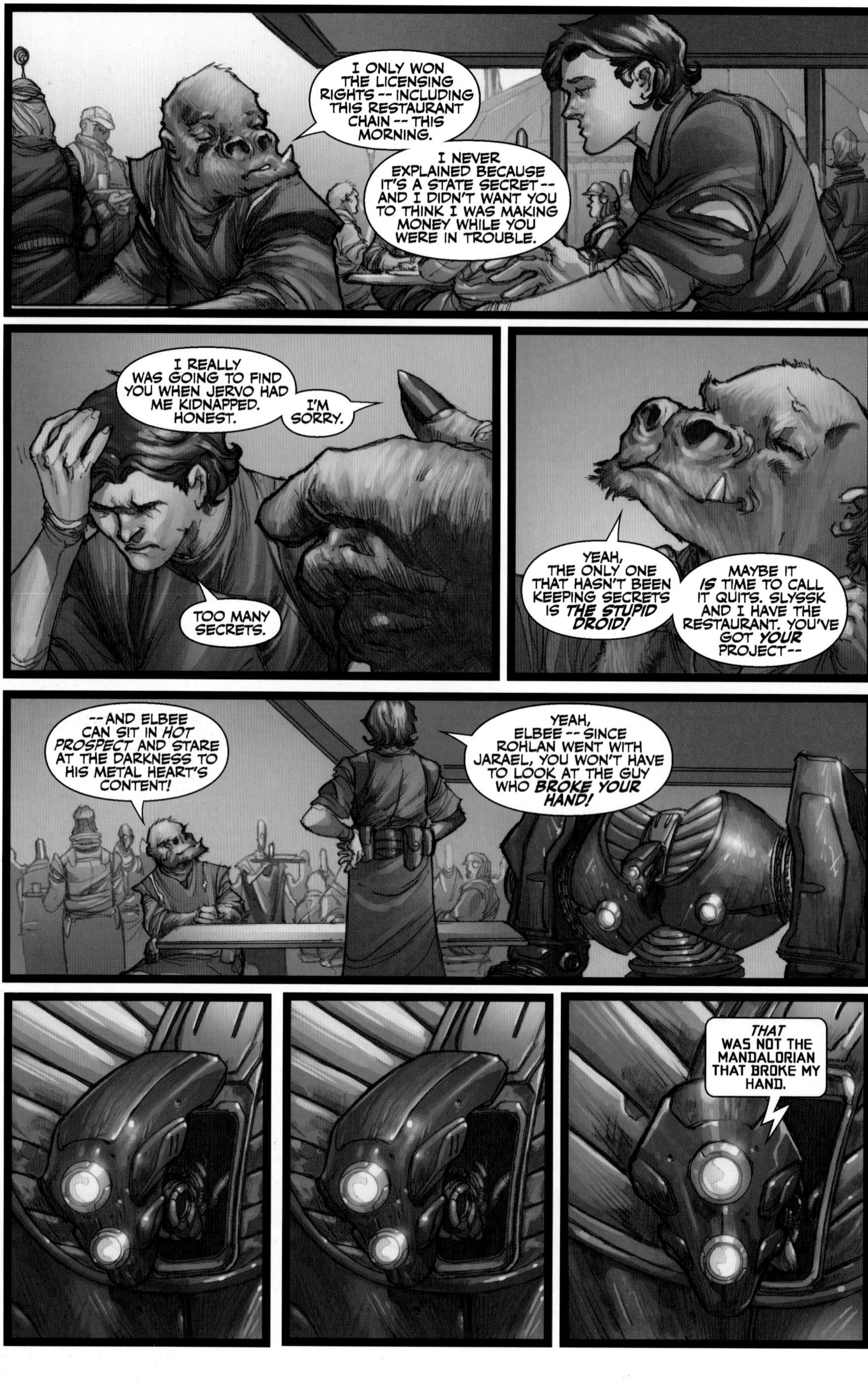
I ONLY WON THE LICENSING RIGHTS -- INCLUDING THIS RESTAURANT CHAIN -- THIS MORNING.
I NEVER EXPLAINED BECAUSE IT'S A STATE SECRET -- AND I DIDN'T WANT YOU TO THINK I WAS MAKING MONEY WHILE YOU WERE IN TROUBLE.
I REALLY WAS GOING TO FIND YOU WHEN JERVO HAD ME KIDNAPPED. HONEST.
I'M SORRY.
TOO MANY SECRETS.
YEAH, THE ONLY ONE THAT HASN'T BEEN KEEPING SECRETS IS *THE STUPID DROID!*
MAYBE IT *IS* TIME TO CALL IT QUITS. SLYSSK AND I HAVE THE RESTAURANT. YOU'VE GOT *YOUR* PROJECT--
--AND ELBEE CAN SIT IN *HOT PROSPECT* AND STARE AT THE DARKNESS TO HIS METAL HEART'S CONTENT!
YEAH, ELBEE -- SINCE ROHLAN WENT WITH JARAEL, YOU WON'T HAVE TO LOOK AT THE GUY WHO *BROKE YOUR HAND!*
THAT WAS NOT THE MANDALORIAN THAT BROKE MY HAND.

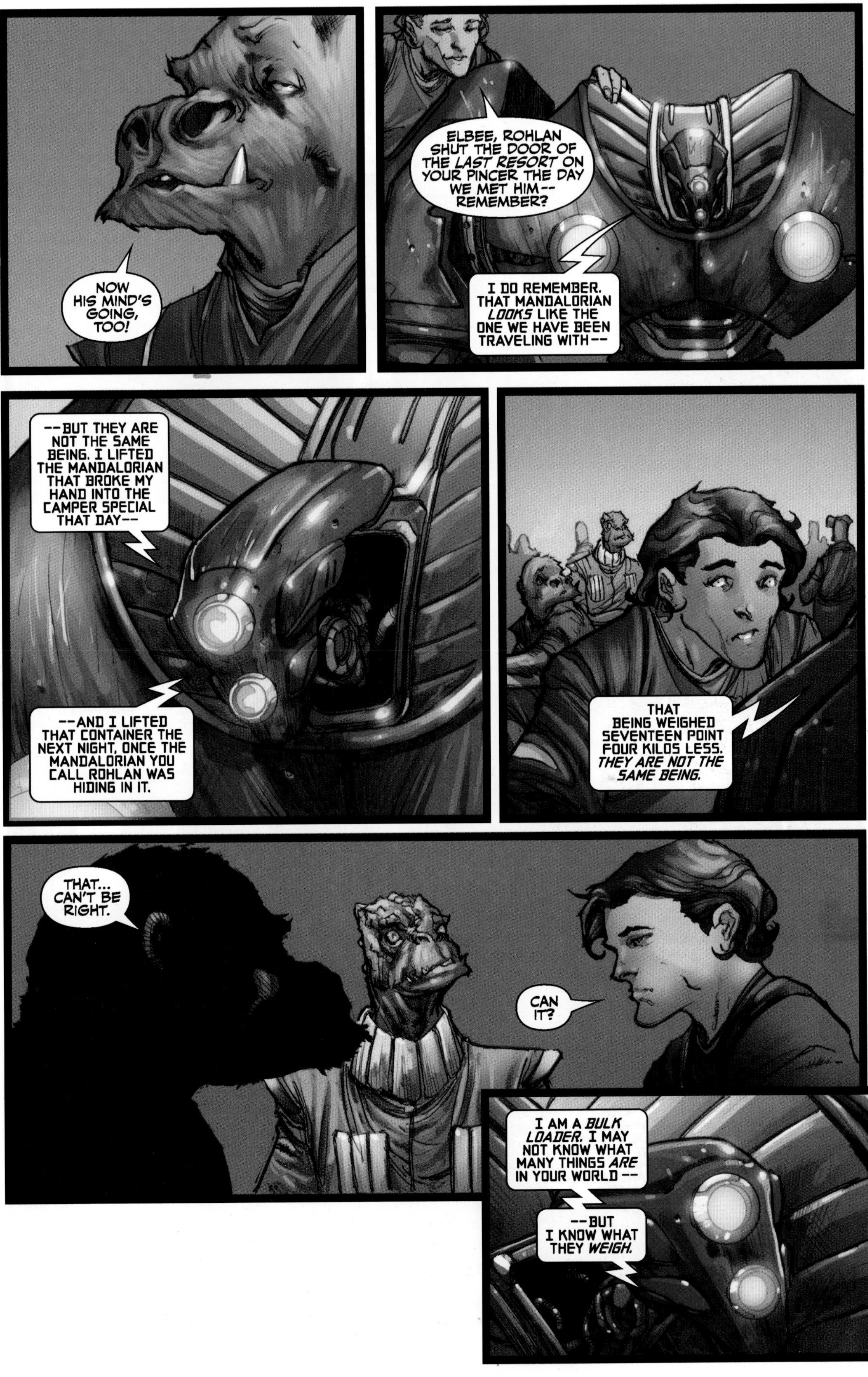
NOW HIS MIND'S GOING, TOO!
ELBEE, ROHLAN SHUT THE DOOR OF THE *LAST RESORT* ON YOUR PINCER THE DAY WE MET HIM--REMEMBER?
I DO REMEMBER. THAT MANDALORIAN *LOOKS* LIKE THE ONE WE HAVE BEEN TRAVELING WITH--
--BUT THEY ARE NOT THE SAME BEING. I LIFTED THE MANDALORIAN THAT BROKE MY HAND INTO THE CAMPER SPECIAL THAT DAY--
--AND I LIFTED THAT CONTAINER THE NEXT NIGHT, ONCE THE MANDALORIAN YOU CALL ROHLAN WAS HIDING IN IT.
THAT BEING WEIGHED SEVENTEEN POINT FOUR KILOS LESS. *THEY ARE NOT THE SAME BEING.*
THAT... CAN'T BE RIGHT.
CAN IT?
I AM A *BULK LOADER*. I MAY NOT KNOW WHAT MANY THINGS *ARE* IN YOUR WORLD --
--BUT I KNOW WHAT THEY *WEIGH*.

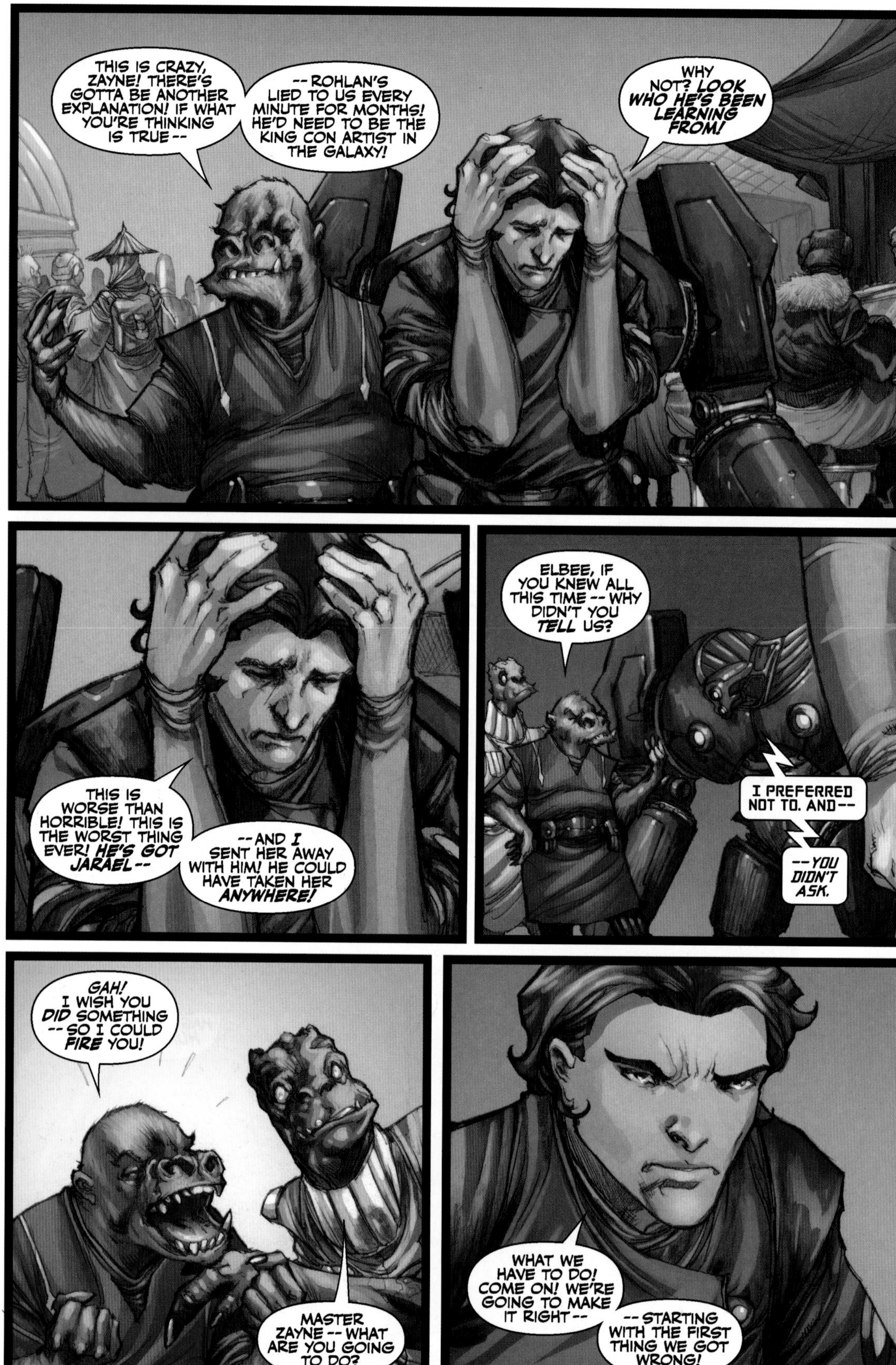
THIS IS CRAZY, ZAYNE! THERE'S GOTTA BE ANOTHER EXPLANATION! IF WHAT YOU'RE THINKING IS TRUE--
--ROHLAN'S LIED TO US EVERY MINUTE FOR MONTHS! HE'D NEED TO BE THE KING CON ARTIST IN THE GALAXY!
WHY NOT? LOOK WHO HE'S BEEN LEARNING FROM!
THIS IS WORSE THAN HORRIBLE! THIS IS THE WORST THING EVER! HE'S GOT JARAEL--
--AND I SENT HER AWAY WITH HIM! HE COULD HAVE TAKEN HER ANYWHERE!
ELBEE, IF YOU KNEW ALL THIS TIME--WHY DIDN'T YOU TELL US?
I PREFERRED NOT TO. AND--
--YOU DIDN'T ASK.
GAH! I WISH YOU DID SOMETHING--SO I COULD FIRE YOU!
MASTER ZAYNE--WHAT ARE YOU GOING TO DO?
WHAT WE HAVE TO DO! COME ON! WE'RE GOING TO MAKE IT RIGHT--
--STARTING WITH THE FIRST THING WE GOT WRONG!

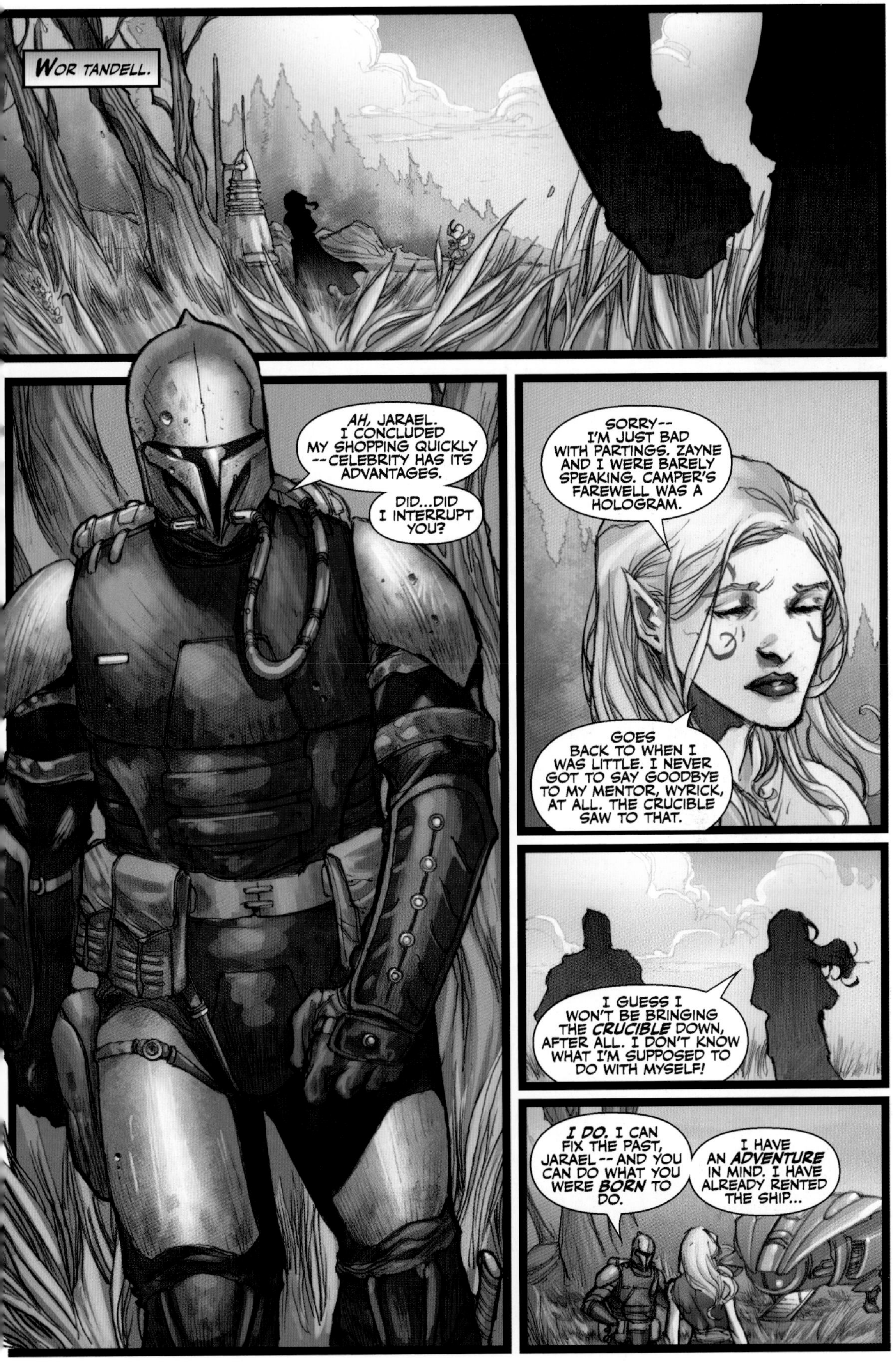
WOR TANDELL.
AH, JARAEL. I CONCLUDED MY SHOPPING QUICKLY --CELEBRITY HAS ITS ADVANTAGES.
DID...DID I INTERRUPT YOU?
SORRY-- I'M JUST BAD WITH PARTINGS. ZAYNE AND I WERE BARELY SPEAKING. CAMPER'S FAREWELL WAS A HOLOGRAM.
GOES BACK TO WHEN I WAS LITTLE. I NEVER GOT TO SAY GOODBYE TO MY MENTOR, WYRICK, AT ALL. THE CRUCIBLE SAW TO THAT.
I GUESS I WON'T BE BRINGING THE CRUCIBLE DOWN, AFTER ALL. I DON'T KNOW WHAT I'M SUPPOSED TO DO WITH MYSELF!
I DO. I CAN FIX THE PAST, JARAEL -- AND YOU CAN DO WHAT YOU WERE BORN TO DO.
I HAVE AN ADVENTURE IN MIND. I HAVE ALREADY RENTED THE SHIP...

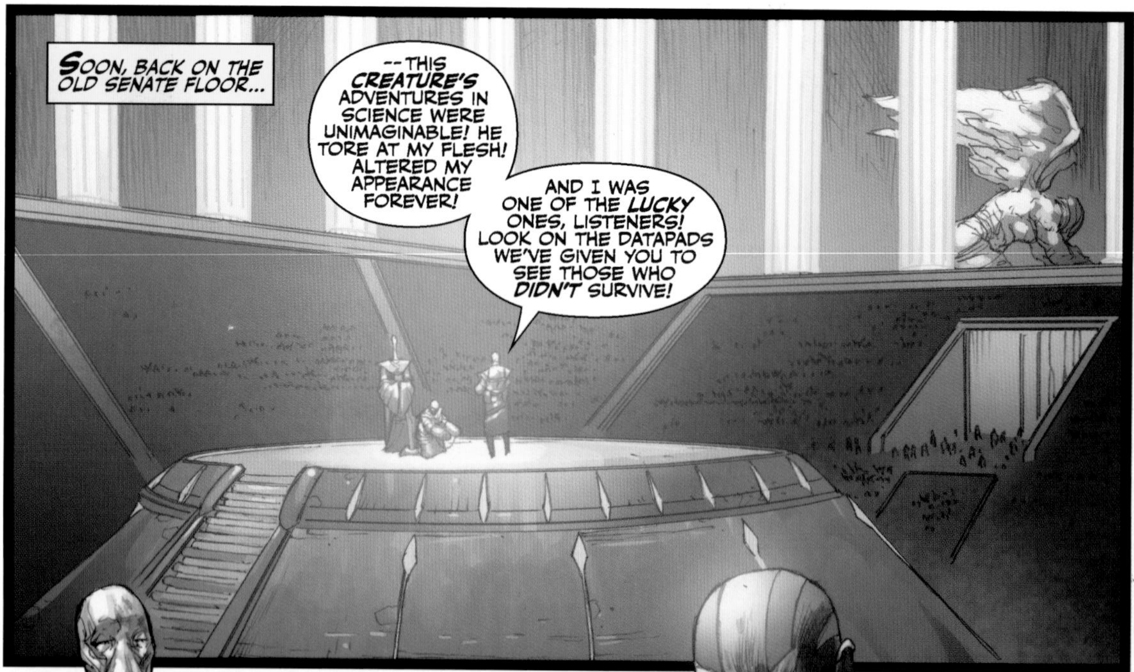
SOON, BACK ON THE OLD SENATE FLOOR...
--THIS CREATURE'S ADVENTURES IN SCIENCE WERE UNIMAGINABLE! HE TORE AT MY FLESH! ALTERED MY APPEARANCE FOREVER!
AND I WAS ONE OF THE LUCKY ONES, LISTENERS! LOOK ON THE DATAPADS WE'VE GIVEN YOU TO SEE THOSE WHO DIDN'T SURVIVE!

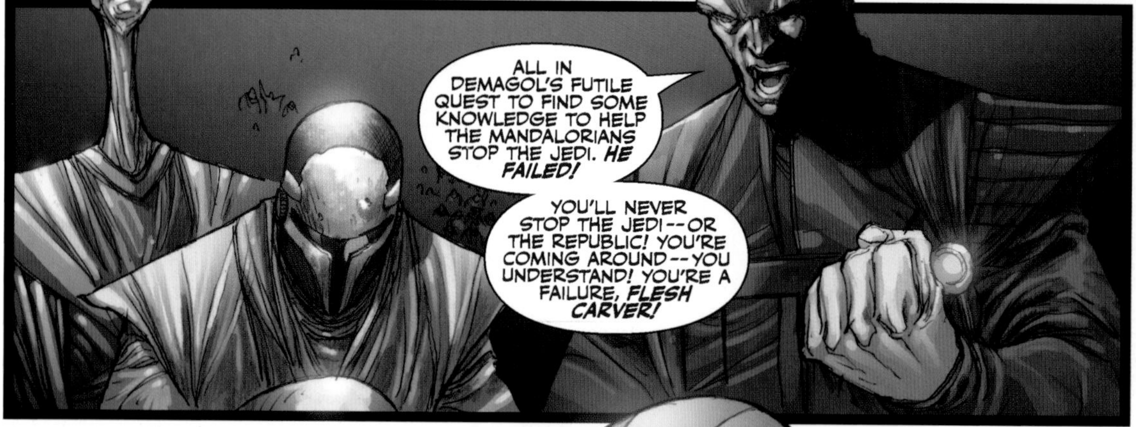
ALL IN DEMAGOL'S FUTILE QUEST TO FIND SOME KNOWLEDGE TO HELP THE MANDALORIANS STOP THE JEDI. HE FAILED!
YOU'LL NEVER STOP THE JEDI--OR THE REPUBLIC! YOU'RE COMING AROUND--YOU UNDERSTAND! YOU'RE A FAILURE, FLESH CARVER!

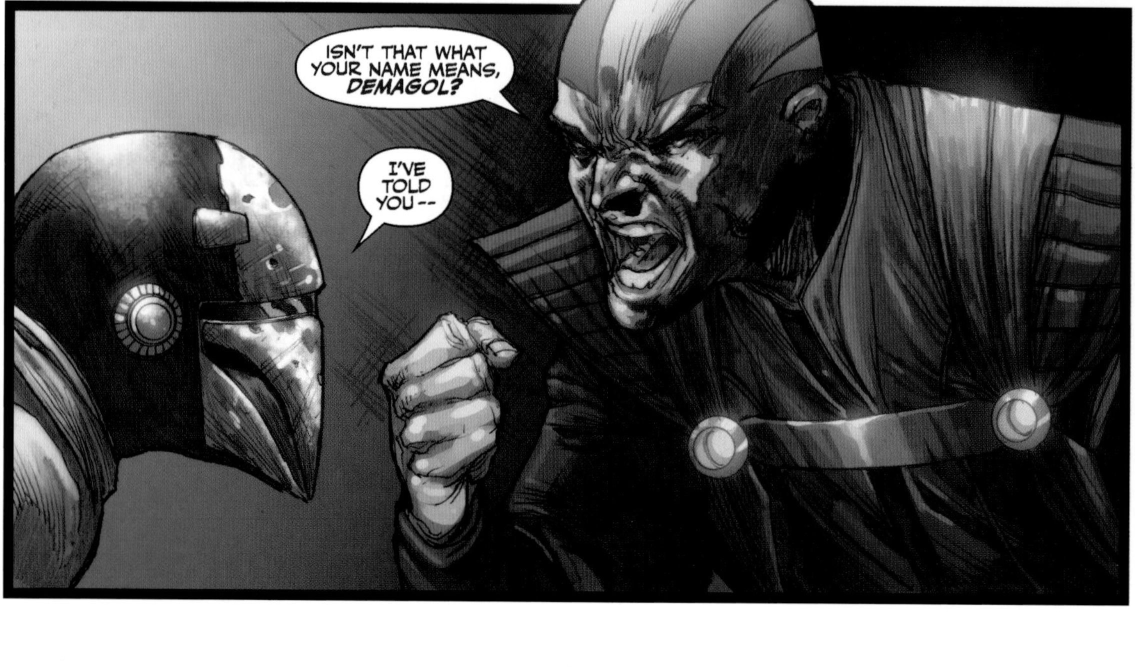
ISN'T THAT WHAT YOUR NAME MEANS, DEMAGOL?
I'VE TOLD YOU--

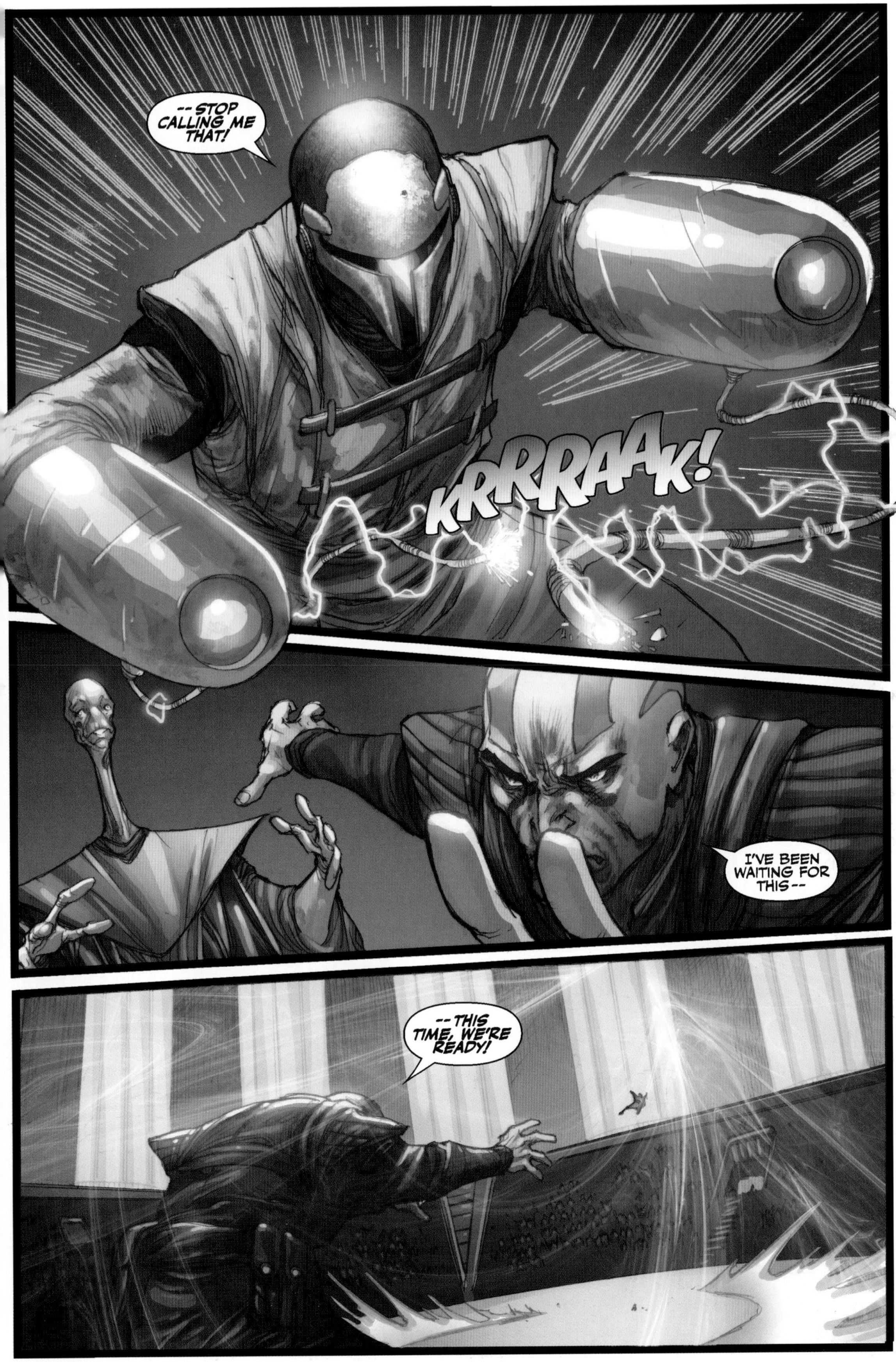
--STOP CALLING ME THAT!
KRRRAAK!
I'VE BEEN WAITING FOR THIS--
--THIS TIME, WE'RE READY!

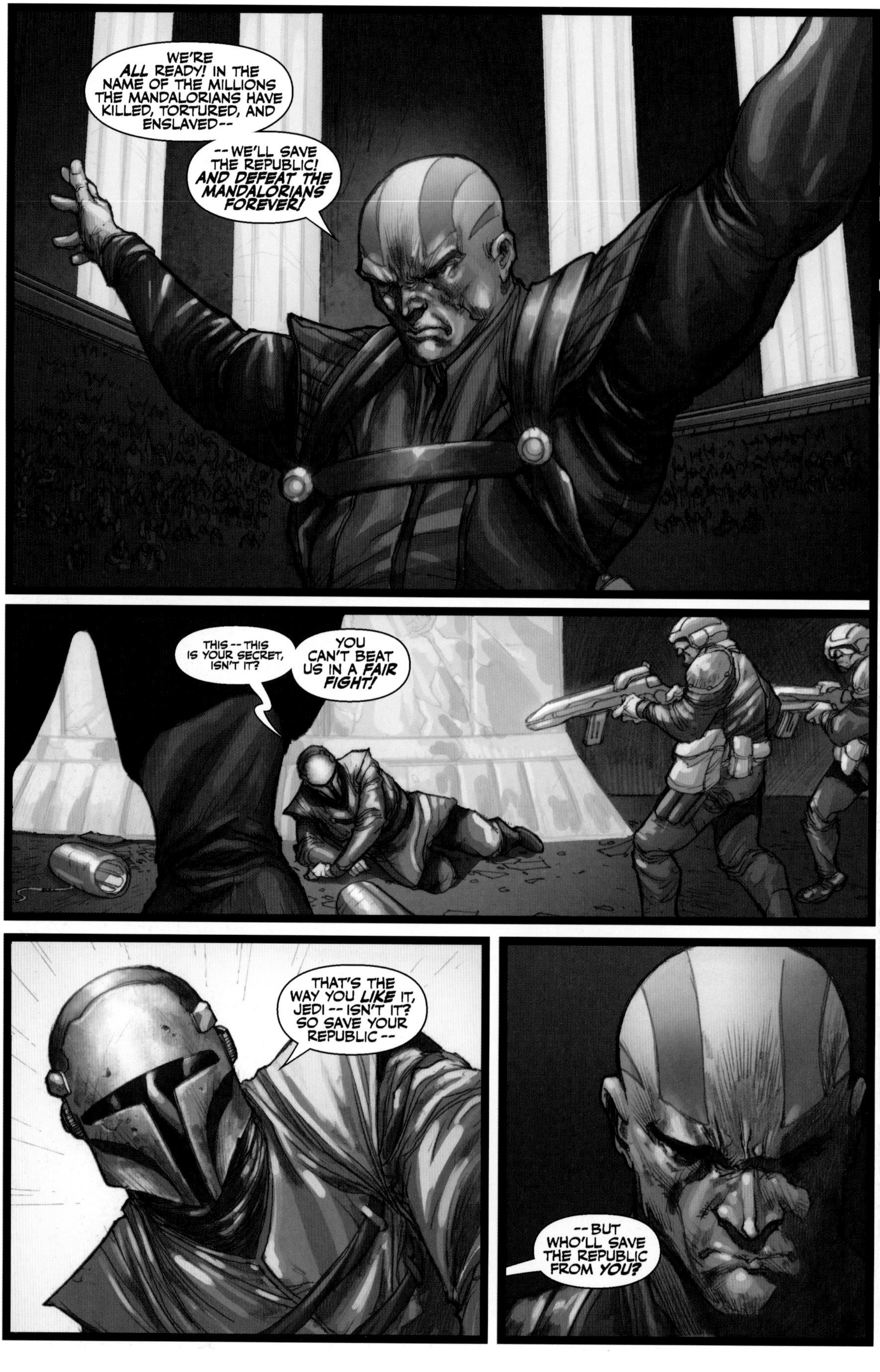
WE'RE ALL READY! IN THE NAME OF THE MILLIONS THE MANDALORIANS HAVE KILLED, TORTURED, AND ENSLAVED--
--WE'LL SAVE THE REPUBLIC! AND DEFEAT THE MANDALORIANS FOREVER!
THIS--THIS IS YOUR SECRET, ISN'T IT?
YOU CAN'T BEAT US IN A FAIR FIGHT!
THAT'S THE WAY YOU LIKE IT, JEDI--ISN'T IT? SO SAVE YOUR REPUBLIC--
--BUT WHO'LL SAVE THE REPUBLIC FROM YOU?

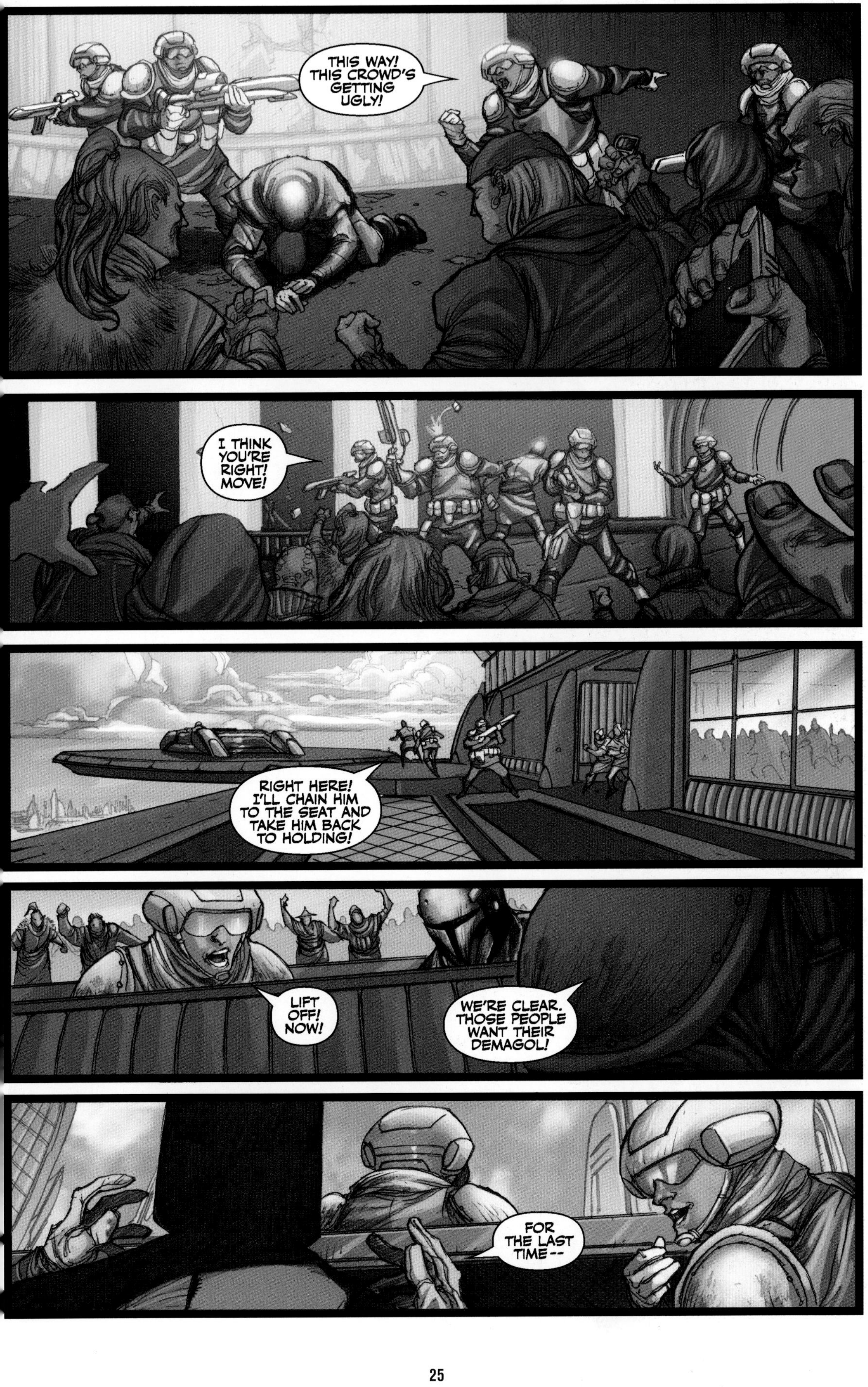
THIS WAY! THIS CROWD'S GETTING UGLY!
I THINK YOU'RE RIGHT! MOVE!
RIGHT HERE! I'LL CHAIN HIM TO THE SEAT AND TAKE HIM BACK TO HOLDING!
LIFT OFF! NOW!
WE'RE CLEAR. THOSE PEOPLE WANT THEIR DEMAGOL!
FOR THE LAST TIME--

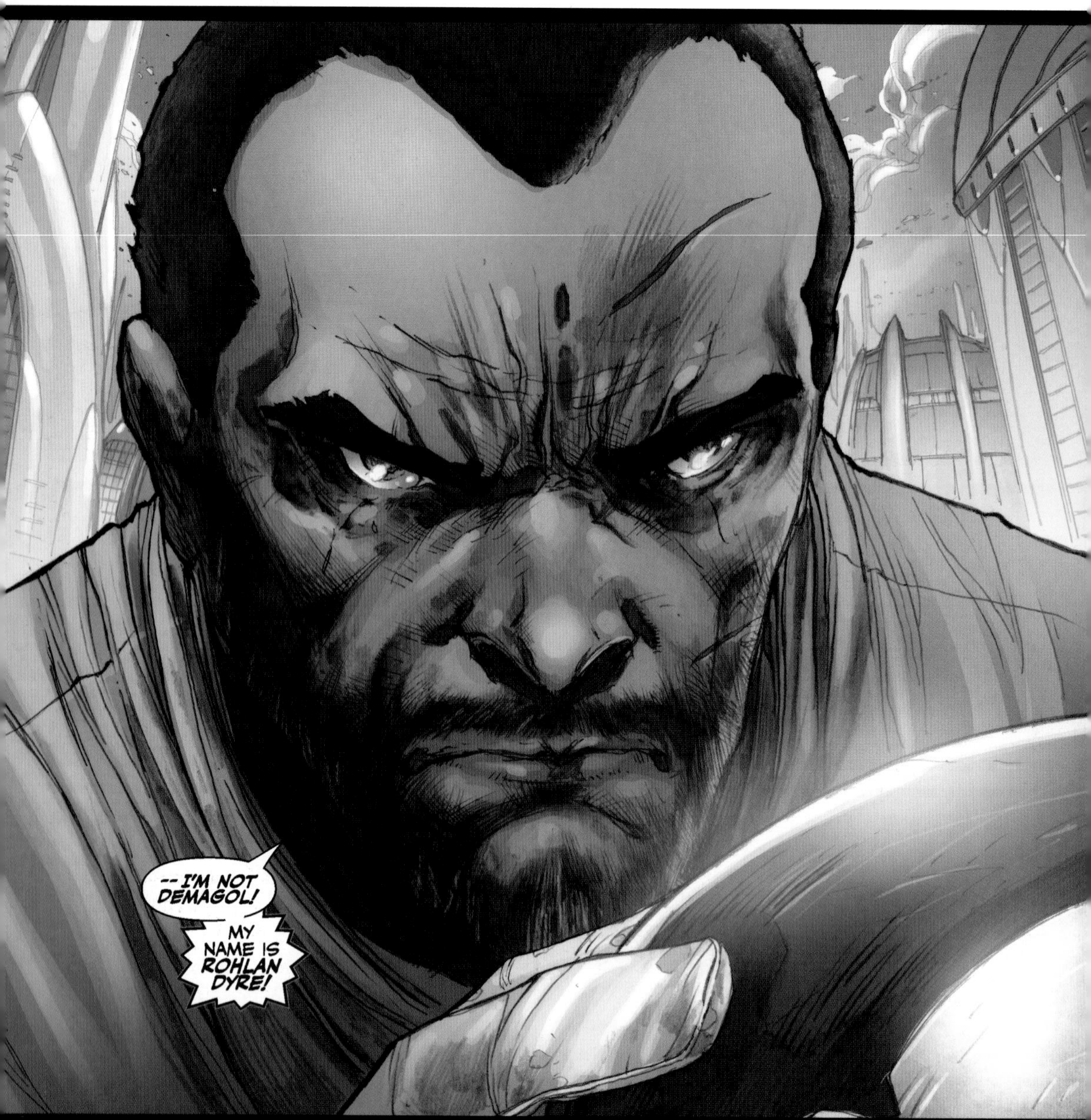
--I'M NOT DEMAGOL!
MY NAME IS ROHLAN DYRE!

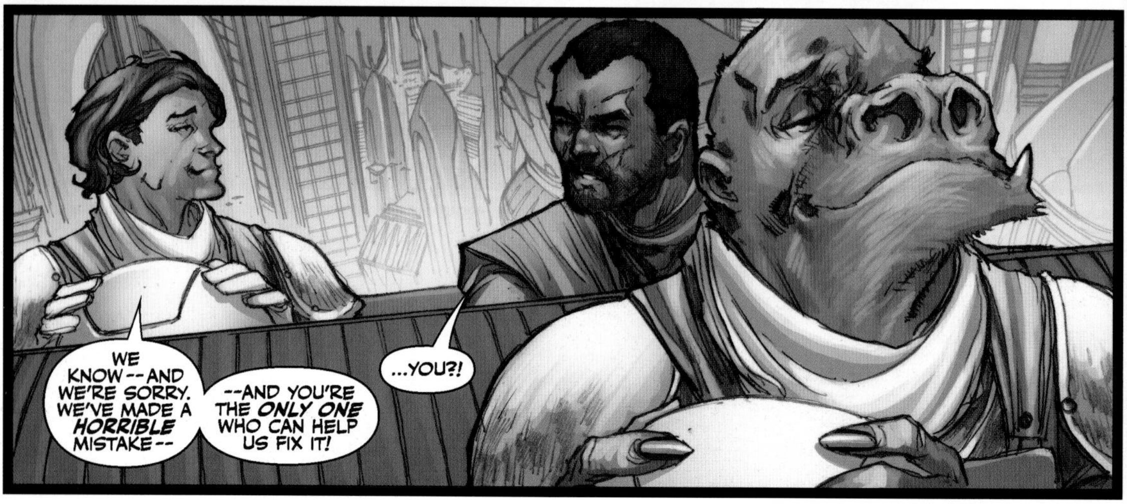
...YOU?!
WE KNOW--AND WE'RE SORRY. WE'VE MADE A *HORRIBLE* MISTAKE--
--AND YOU'RE THE *ONLY ONE* WHO CAN HELP US FIX IT!

HYPERSPACE. DESTINATION... UNKNOWN.

JARAEL, YOU SAID YOUR SCHOOLMATES WERE ALSO KIDNAPPED BY *THE CRUCIBLE.* BEFORE WE PARTED, CARRICK SAID THEY YET LIVED--

--AND THAT THE SLAVERS HAD HIDDEN THEM SOMEPLACE *IRONIC.* THAT WAS ALL HE KNEW. NOW, WHERE WOULD THEY CONSIDER *IRONIC?*

I--I DON'T...

...OSADIA?

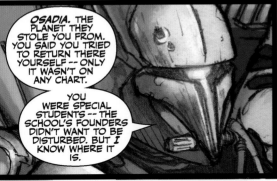

OSADIA. THE PLANET THEY STOLE YOU FROM. YOU SAID YOU TRIED TO RETURN THERE YOURSELF -- ONLY IT WASN'T ON ANY CHART.

YOU WERE SPECIAL STUDENTS -- THE SCHOOL'S FOUNDERS DIDN'T WANT TO BE DISTURBED. BUT *I* KNOW WHERE IT IS.

THAT'S GREAT! I--

-- WAIT. ROHLAN, HOW COULD *YOU* KNOW ABOUT MY SCHOOL?

I KNOW EVERYTHING. I WAS PRESENT AT YOUR BIRTH. I WATCHED YOU GROW AND LEARN THEN --AND NOW.

MY EDESSA. MY TRIUMPH.

PERERO?

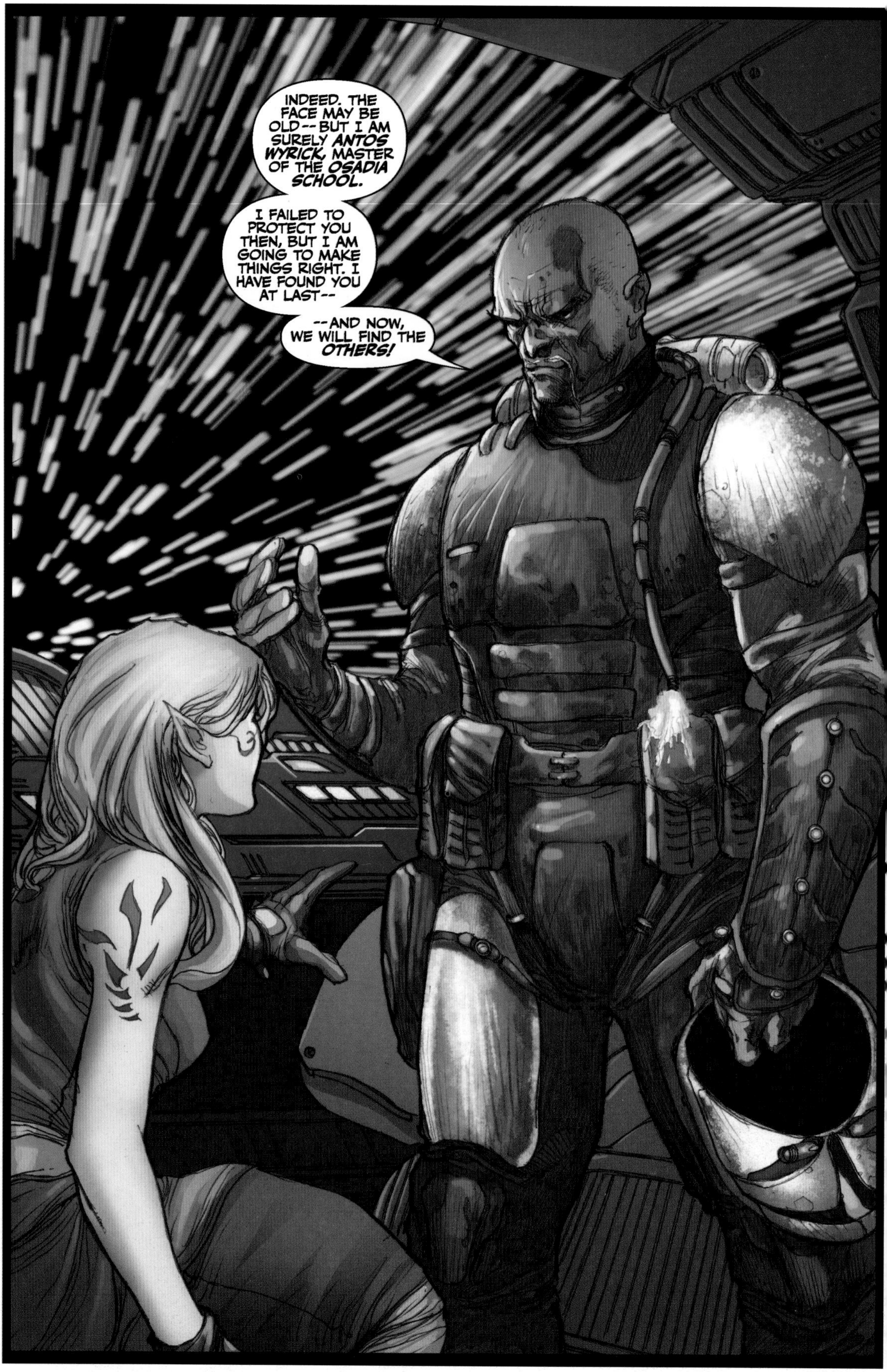
INDEED. THE FACE MAY BE OLD--BUT I AM SURELY ANTOS WYRICK, MASTER OF THE OSADIA SCHOOL.
I FAILED TO PROTECT YOU THEN, BUT I AM GOING TO MAKE THINGS RIGHT. I HAVE FOUND YOU AT LAST--
--AND NOW, WE WILL FIND THE OTHERS!

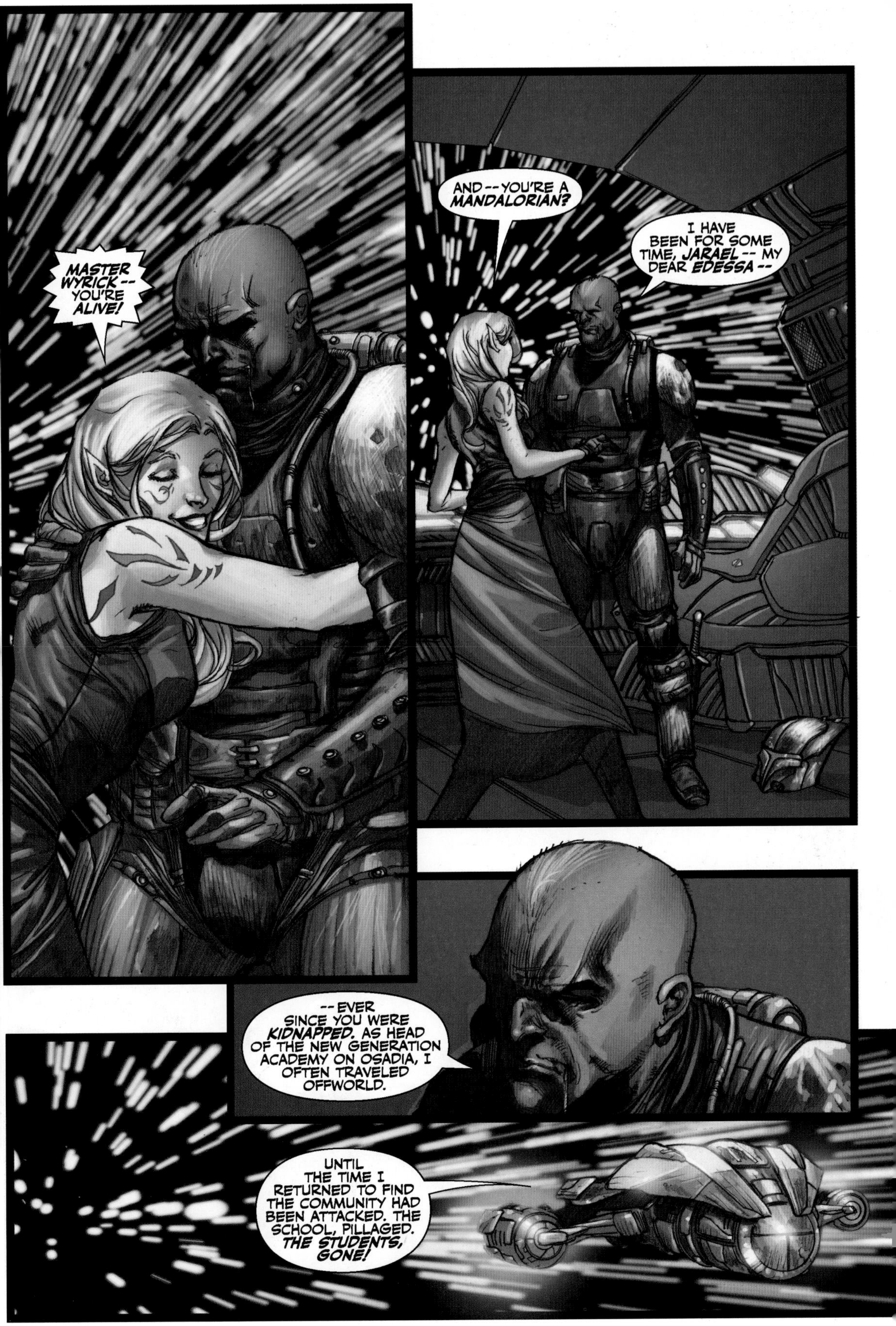
MASTER WYRICK -- YOU'RE ALIVE!
AND -- YOU'RE A MANDALORIAN?
I HAVE BEEN FOR SOME TIME, JARAEL -- MY DEAR EDESSA --
-- EVER SINCE YOU WERE KIDNAPPED. AS HEAD OF THE NEW GENERATION ACADEMY ON OSADIA, I OFTEN TRAVELED OFFWORLD.
UNTIL THE TIME I RETURNED TO FIND THE COMMUNITY HAD BEEN ATTACKED. THE SCHOOL, PILLAGED. THE STUDENTS, GONE!

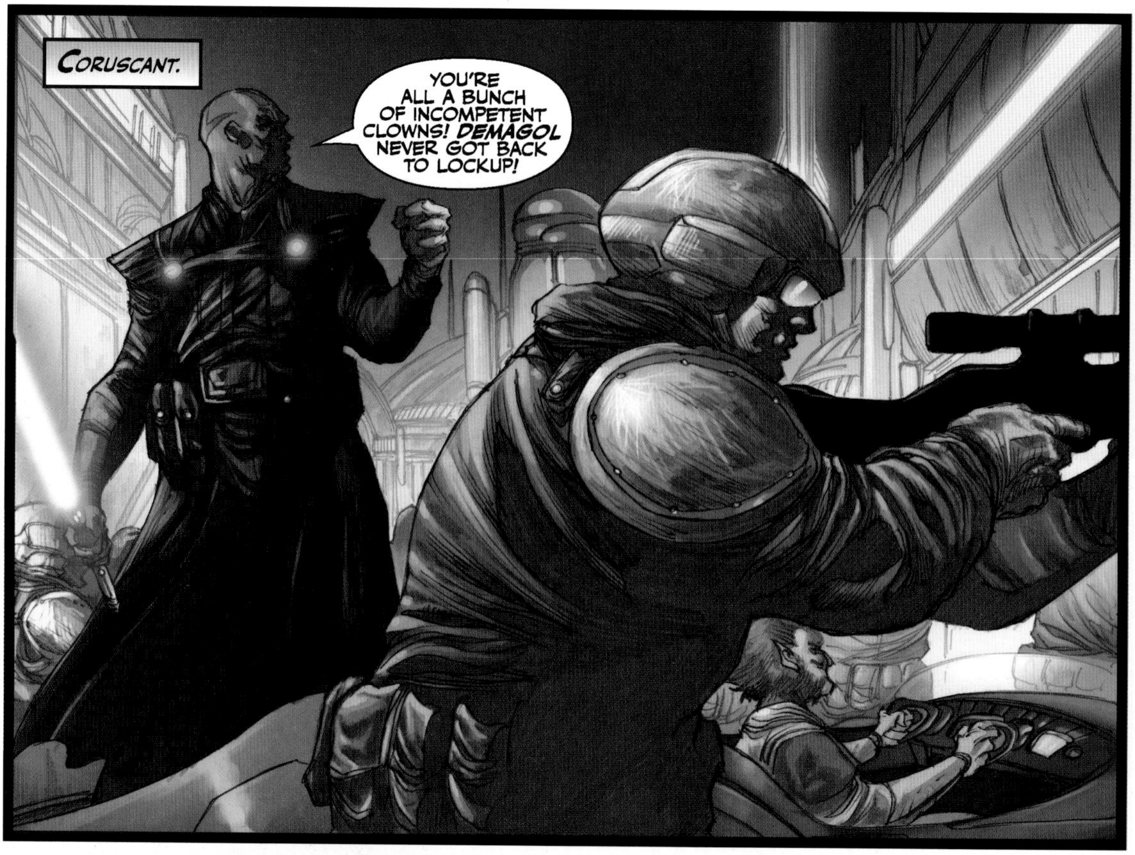
CORUSCANT.
YOU'RE ALL A BUNCH OF INCOMPETENT CLOWNS! DEMAGOL NEVER GOT BACK TO LOCKUP!

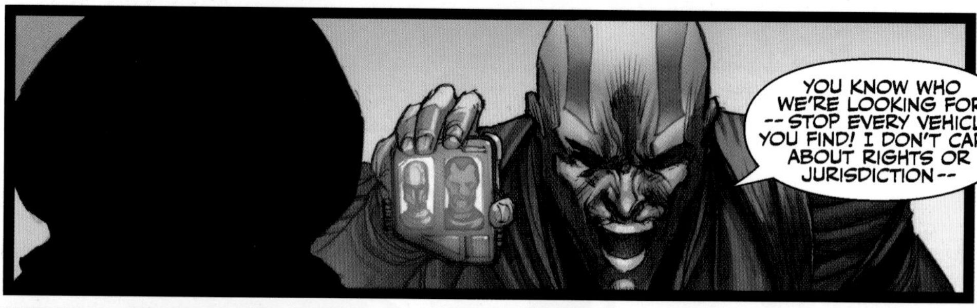
YOU KNOW WHO WE'RE LOOKING FOR -- STOP EVERY VEHICLE YOU FIND! I DON'T CARE ABOUT RIGHTS OR JURISDICTION --

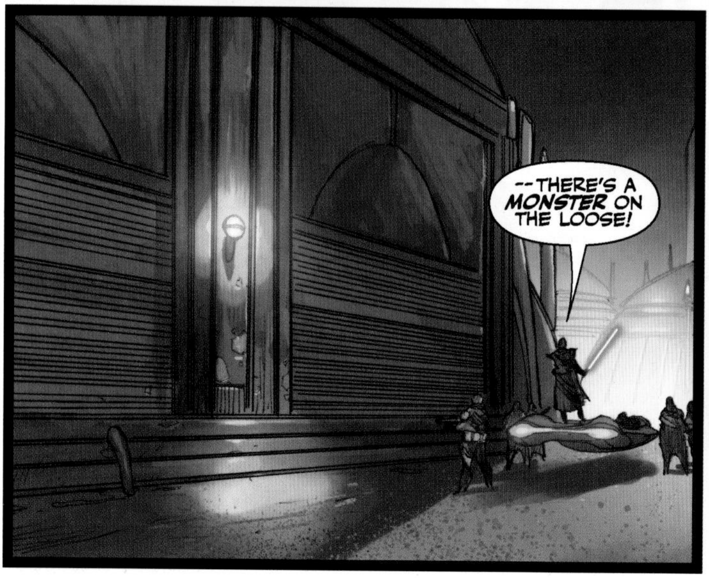
-- THERE'S A MONSTER ON THE LOOSE!

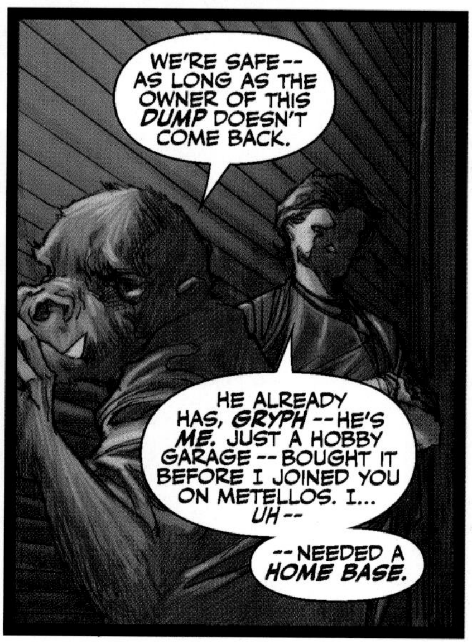
WE'RE SAFE -- AS LONG AS THE OWNER OF THIS DUMP DOESN'T COME BACK.
HE ALREADY HAS, GRYPH -- HE'S ME. JUST A HOBBY GARAGE -- BOUGHT IT BEFORE I JOINED YOU ON METELLOS. I... UH --
-- NEEDED A HOME BASE.

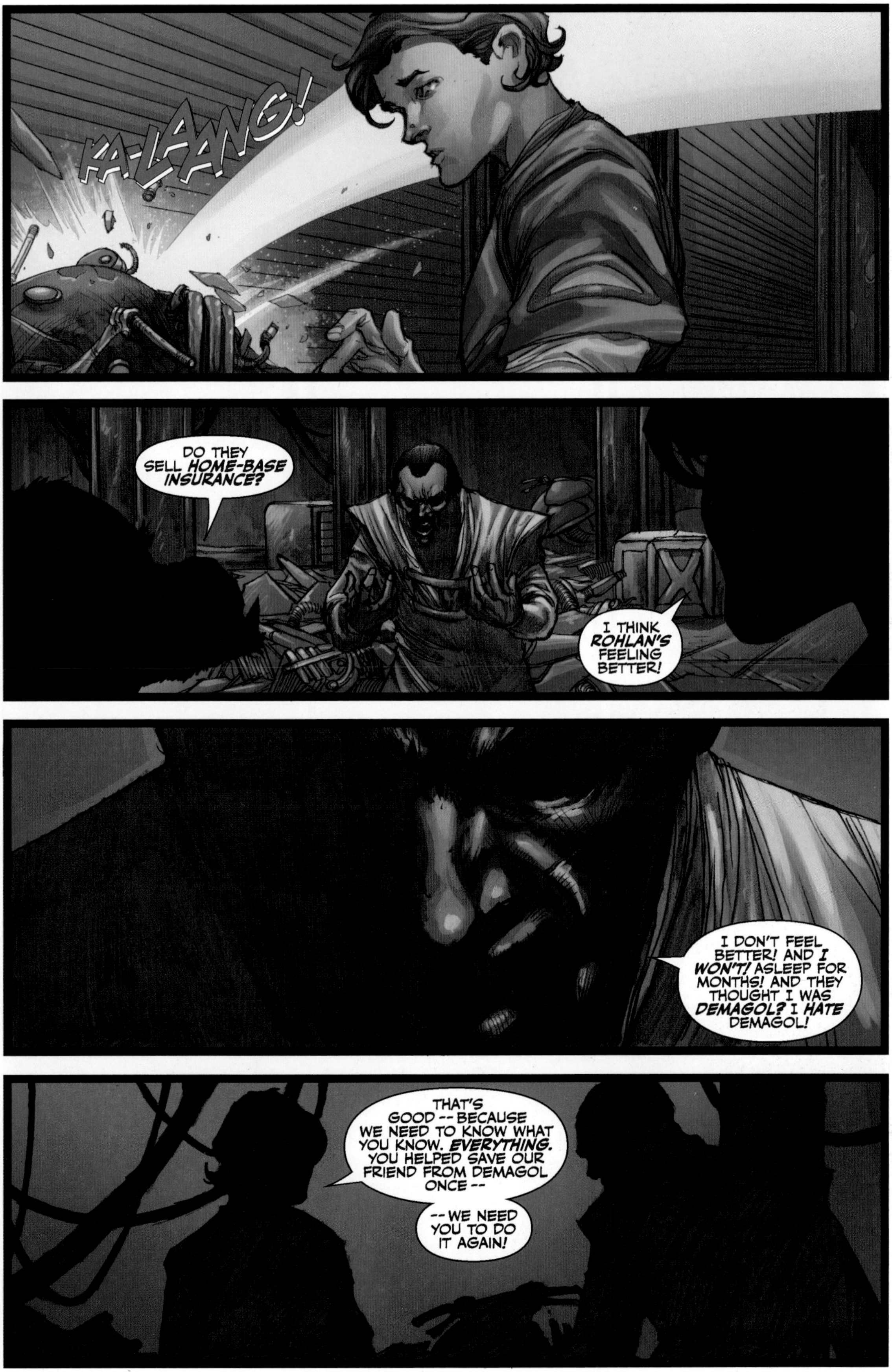
KA-LAANG!
DO THEY SELL HOME-BASE INSURANCE?
I THINK ROHLAN'S FEELING BETTER!
I DON'T FEEL BETTER! AND I WON'T! ASLEEP FOR MONTHS! AND THEY THOUGHT I WAS DEMAGOL? I HATE DEMAGOL!
THAT'S GOOD -- BECAUSE WE NEED TO KNOW WHAT YOU KNOW. EVERYTHING. YOU HELPED SAVE OUR FRIEND FROM DEMAGOL ONCE --
-- WE NEED YOU TO DO IT AGAIN!

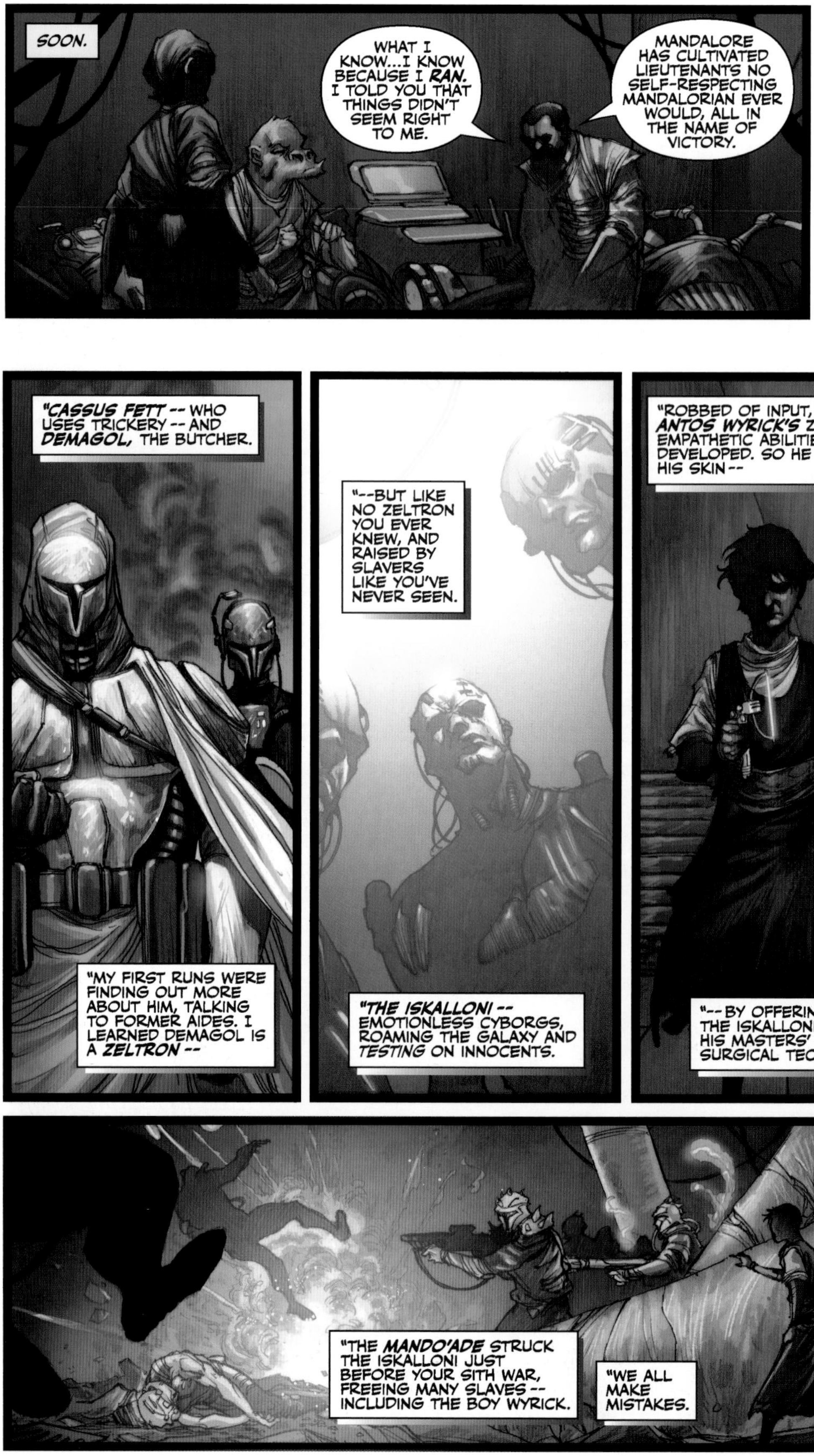
SOON.
WHAT I KNOW...I KNOW BECAUSE I RAN. I TOLD YOU THAT THINGS DIDN'T SEEM RIGHT TO ME.
MANDALORE HAS CULTIVATED LIEUTENANTS NO SELF-RESPECTING MANDALORIAN EVER WOULD, ALL IN THE NAME OF VICTORY.
"CASSUS FETT -- WHO USES TRICKERY -- AND DEMAGOL, THE BUTCHER.
"MY FIRST RUNS WERE FINDING OUT MORE ABOUT HIM, TALKING TO FORMER AIDES. I LEARNED DEMAGOL IS A ZELTRON --
"--BUT LIKE NO ZELTRON YOU EVER KNEW, AND RAISED BY SLAVERS LIKE YOU'VE NEVER SEEN.
"THE ISKALLONI -- EMOTIONLESS CYBORGS, ROAMING THE GALAXY AND TESTING ON INNOCENTS.
"ROBBED OF INPUT, YOUNG ANTOS WYRICK'S ZELTRON EMPATHETIC ABILITIES NEVER DEVELOPED. SO HE SAVED HIS SKIN --
"-- BY OFFERING TO HELP THE ISKALLONI, LEARNING HIS MASTERS' HIDEOUS SURGICAL TECHNIQUES.
"THE MANDO'ADE STRUCK THE ISKALLONI JUST BEFORE YOUR SITH WAR, FREEING MANY SLAVES -- INCLUDING THE BOY WYRICK.
"WE ALL MAKE MISTAKES.

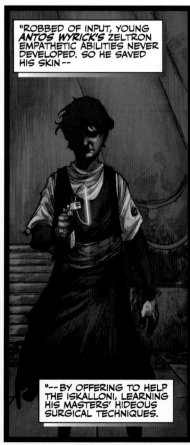

"OUR MEDICS TAUGHT HIM ABOUT OTHER SPECIES -- AND *MANDALORE THE INDOMITABLE* HIMSELF TAUGHT HIM MARTIAL ARTS.

"SO HE WAS STUNNED WHEN THE DARK JEDI *ULIC QEL-DROMA* BESTED THE INDOMITABLE IN SINGLE COMBAT, SUBJUGATING THE MANDO'ADE.

"HOW WAS IT POSSIBLE? WHAT WAS INSIDE THE JEDI? HE HAD TO KNOW.

"LATER, WYRICK SEARCHED ULIC'S CABIN FOR ANYTHING THAT MIGHT PROVIDE ANSWERS. HE FOUND SOMETHING --

"-- A *ROBE* THAT ULIC ALWAYS CARRIED WITH HIM. PERHAPS IT HELD SOME GENETIC TRACE THAT WOULD REVEAL MORE ABOUT THE JEDI.

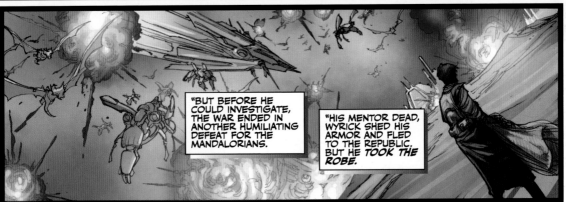

"BUT BEFORE HE COULD INVESTIGATE, THE WAR ENDED IN ANOTHER HUMILIATING DEFEAT FOR THE MANDALORIANS.

"HIS MENTOR DEAD, WYRICK SHED HIS ARMOR AND FLED TO THE REPUBLIC. BUT HE *TOOK THE ROBE.*

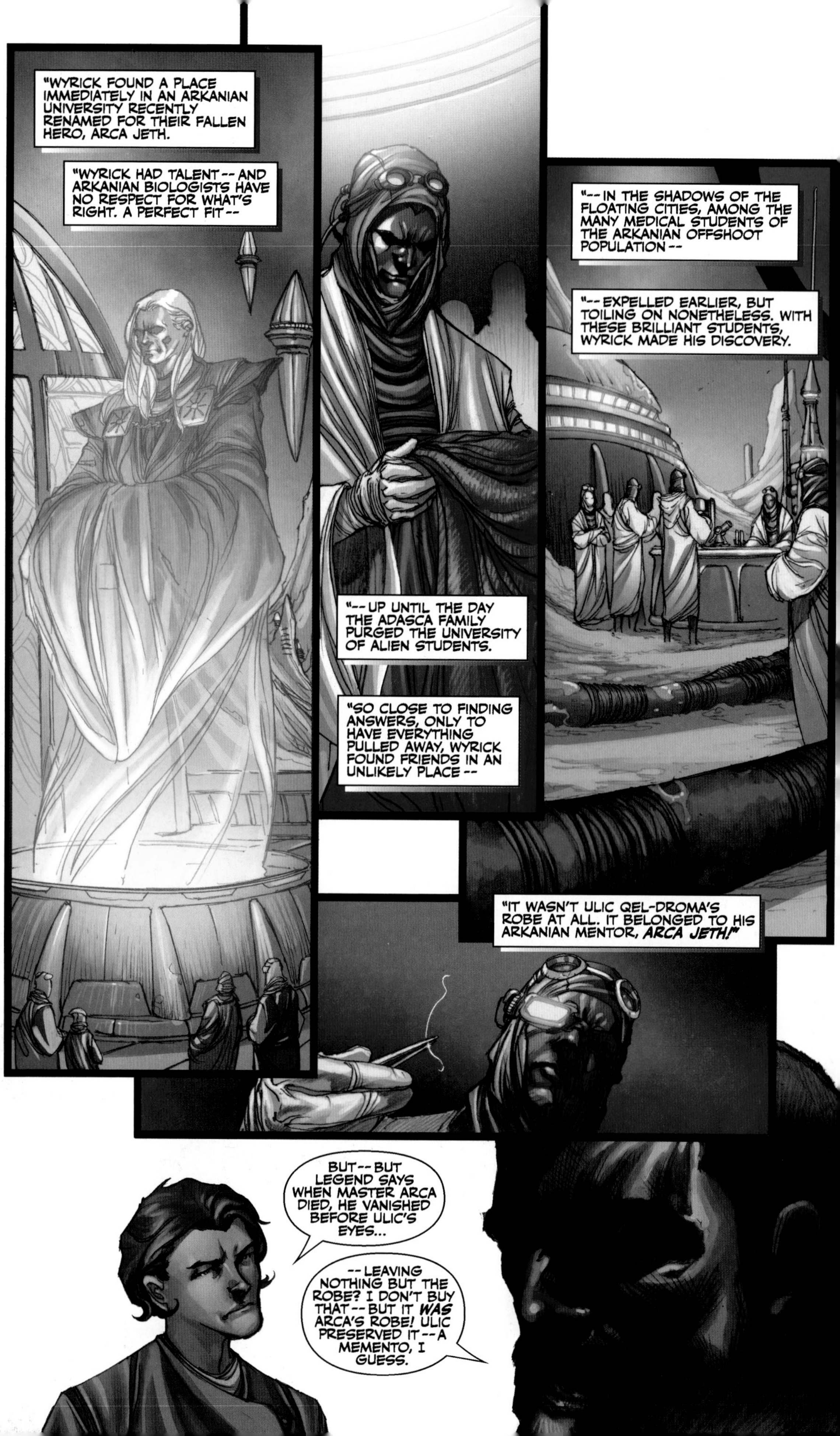
"WYRICK FOUND A PLACE IMMEDIATELY IN AN ARKANIAN UNIVERSITY RECENTLY RENAMED FOR THEIR FALLEN HERO, ARCA JETH.
"WYRICK HAD TALENT-- AND ARKANIAN BIOLOGISTS HAVE NO RESPECT FOR WHAT'S RIGHT. A PERFECT FIT--
"--UP UNTIL THE DAY THE ADASCA FAMILY PURGED THE UNIVERSITY OF ALIEN STUDENTS.
"SO CLOSE TO FINDING ANSWERS, ONLY TO HAVE EVERYTHING PULLED AWAY, WYRICK FOUND FRIENDS IN AN UNLIKELY PLACE--
"--IN THE SHADOWS OF THE FLOATING CITIES, AMONG THE MANY MEDICAL STUDENTS OF THE ARKANIAN OFFSHOOT POPULATION--
"--EXPELLED EARLIER, BUT TOILING ON NONETHELESS. WITH THESE BRILLIANT STUDENTS, WYRICK MADE HIS DISCOVERY.
"IT WASN'T ULIC QEL-DROMA'S ROBE AT ALL. IT BELONGED TO HIS ARKANIAN MENTOR, ARCA JETH!"
BUT-- BUT LEGEND SAYS WHEN MASTER ARCA DIED, HE VANISHED BEFORE ULIC'S EYES...
--LEAVING NOTHING BUT THE ROBE? I DON'T BUY THAT-- BUT IT WAS ARCA'S ROBE! ULIC PRESERVED IT-- A MEMENTO, I GUESS.

"HE HAD GENETIC TRACES OF THE GREAT ARKANIAN JEDI -- BUT WITHOUT BETTER FACILITIES, IT WAS USELESS. HE NEEDED PATRONAGE--

"-- AND FOUND IT, FROM MANDALORIANS INTERESTED IN AVENGING THEIR DEFEAT AT THE HANDS OF THE JEDI.

"WITH THE MANDO'ADE, THE WRONGED OFFSHOOTS COULD PURSUE SCIENCE AS THEY NEVER COULD ON ARKANIA--

"--WHILE MAKING THE CELLS OF ARKANIA'S GREATEST HERO WORK FOR THEIR OWN PURPOSES!

"WITH THEM AND OTHER VOLUNTEERS, WYRICK FORMED A RESEARCH COLONY ON A HIDDEN PLANET -- OSADIA.

"IT LOOKED LIKE A UTOPIAN COMMUNITY FAR FROM THE REPUBLIC AND ITS WARS--

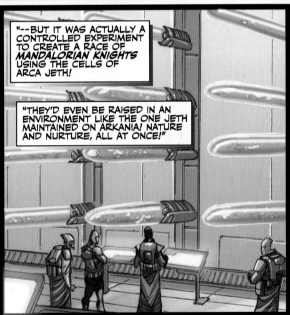

"--BUT IT WAS ACTUALLY A CONTROLLED EXPERIMENT TO CREATE A RACE OF MANDALORIAN KNIGHTS USING THE CELLS OF ARCA JETH!

"THEY'D EVEN BE RAISED IN AN ENVIRONMENT LIKE THE ONE JETH MAINTAINED ON ARKANIA! NATURE AND NURTURE, ALL AT ONCE!

IS THAT EVEN POSSIBLE? YOU CAN'T GROW JEDI!

NEITHER COULD THEY--

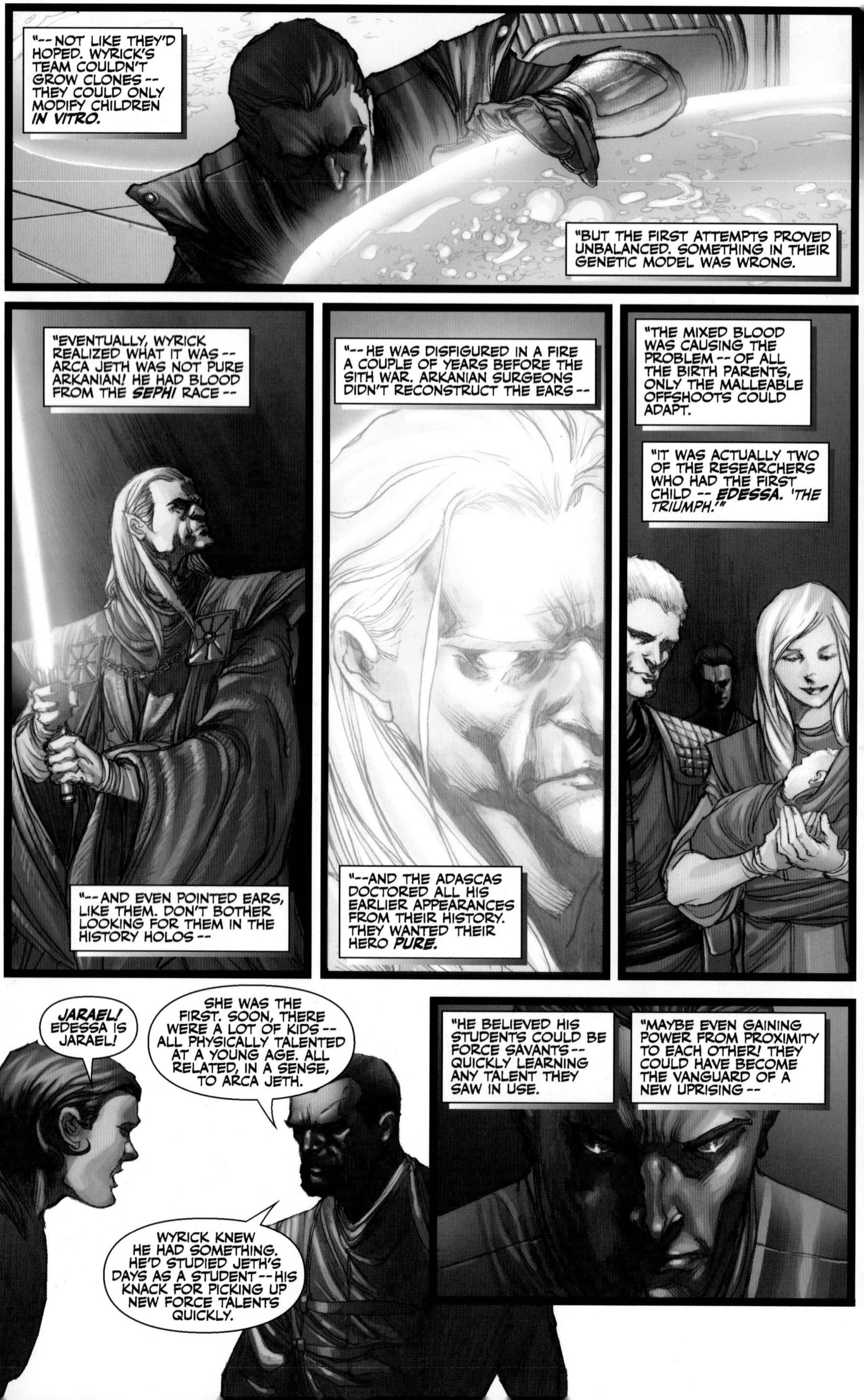
"--NOT LIKE THEY'D HOPED. WYRICK'S TEAM COULDN'T GROW CLONES--THEY COULD ONLY MODIFY CHILDREN *IN VITRO.*
"BUT THE FIRST ATTEMPTS PROVED UNBALANCED. SOMETHING IN THEIR GENETIC MODEL WAS WRONG.
"EVENTUALLY, WYRICK REALIZED WHAT IT WAS--ARCA JETH WAS NOT PURE ARKANIAN! HE HAD BLOOD FROM THE *SEPHI* RACE--
"--AND EVEN POINTED EARS, LIKE THEM. DON'T BOTHER LOOKING FOR THEM IN THE HISTORY HOLOS--
"--HE WAS DISFIGURED IN A FIRE A COUPLE OF YEARS BEFORE THE SITH WAR. ARKANIAN SURGEONS DIDN'T RECONSTRUCT THE EARS--
"--AND THE ADASCAS DOCTORED ALL HIS EARLIER APPEARANCES FROM THEIR HISTORY. THEY WANTED THEIR HERO *PURE.*
"THE MIXED BLOOD WAS CAUSING THE PROBLEM--OF ALL THE BIRTH PARENTS, ONLY THE MALLEABLE OFFSHOOTS COULD ADAPT.
"IT WAS ACTUALLY TWO OF THE RESEARCHERS WHO HAD THE FIRST CHILD--*EDESSA.* '*THE TRIUMPH.*'"
JARAEL! EDESSA IS JARAEL!
SHE WAS THE FIRST. SOON, THERE WERE A LOT OF KIDS--ALL PHYSICALLY TALENTED AT A YOUNG AGE. ALL RELATED, IN A SENSE, TO ARCA JETH.
WYRICK KNEW HE HAD SOMETHING. HE'D STUDIED JETH'S DAYS AS A STUDENT--HIS KNACK FOR PICKING UP NEW FORCE TALENTS QUICKLY.
"HE BELIEVED HIS STUDENTS COULD BE FORCE SAVANTS--QUICKLY LEARNING ANY TALENT THEY SAW IN USE.
"MAYBE EVEN GAINING POWER FROM PROXIMITY TO EACH OTHER! THEY COULD HAVE BECOME THE VANGUARD OF A NEW UPRISING--

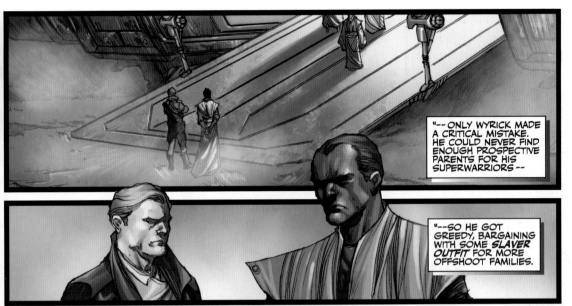

"-- ONLY WYRICK MADE A CRITICAL MISTAKE. HE COULD NEVER FIND ENOUGH PROSPECTIVE PARENTS FOR HIS SUPERWARRIORS --

"--SO HE GOT GREEDY, BARGAINING WITH SOME *SLAVER OUTFIT* FOR MORE OFFSHOOT FAMILIES.

"HE DIDN'T COUNT ON THE SLAVERS BEING GREEDY, TOO. RETURNING FROM A TRIP TO REPORT THEIR SUCCESS TO MANDALORE --

"-- WYRICK AND HIS AIDES RETURNED TO FIND THE GUARDS DEAD, THE LAB RANSACKED -- AND THE CHILDREN *GONE.*

"EVERYTHING CAME APART. HE'D LOST HIS DISCOVERY -- BUT HIS COLLEAGUES HAD LOST THEIR *CHILDREN.*

"WHEN THEY LEARNED *HE'D* BROUGHT THE SLAVERS TO OSADIA, THEY WANTED NOTHING MORE TO DO WITH HIM.

"HIS PROJECT DIED -- BUT SOMETHING AWFUL HAD BEEN BORN. WYRICK RETURNED TO MANDALORE COLDER THAN EVER --

"-- WILLING TO DO ANYTHING TO ANYONE TO ADVANCE HIS SCIENCE. IN TIME, WE CALLED HIM *DEMAR'AGOL* -- THE FLESH CARVER.

"*DEMAGOL.*

"DEMAGOL'S STORY KNOWN, I HAD BEGUN TO LOOK INTO *FETT* -- WHEN I MET *YOU.* I DIDN'T MIND HELPING YOU PUT ONE OVER ON DEMAGOL.

"I STRIPPED HIS ARMOR FOR YOU TO WEAR AT FLASHPOINT. SEEING HE WAS A ZELTRON CONFIRMED WHAT I ALREADY KNEW--

"-- BUT WHEN I RETURNED TO FETCH HIM LATER, I MADE A ROOKIE MISTAKE. *NEVER REMOVE YOUR HELMET WHILE THE HOSTILE'S BREATHING.*

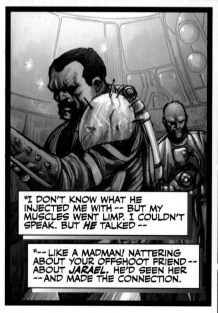

"I DON'T KNOW WHAT HE INJECTED ME WITH -- BUT MY MUSCLES WENT LIMP. I COULDN'T SPEAK. BUT *HE* TALKED --

"-- LIKE A MADMAN! NATTERING ABOUT YOUR OFFSHOOT FRIEND-- ABOUT *JAREL.* HE'D SEEN HER --AND MADE THE CONNECTION.

"SHE MIGHT BE A JETH CHILD. AND IF SHE WERE -- THE REST MIGHT YET LIVE, TOO. HE HAD TO GO WITH HER --

"-- AND THAT MEANT HE HAD TO BE *ME.*

"THE LAST THING I REMEMBER WAS ABOARD THE JEDI SHUTTLE. HE DOSED ME AGAIN -- AND AGAIN.

"THEN HE WAS GONE. AND SO WAS EVERYTHING ELSE."

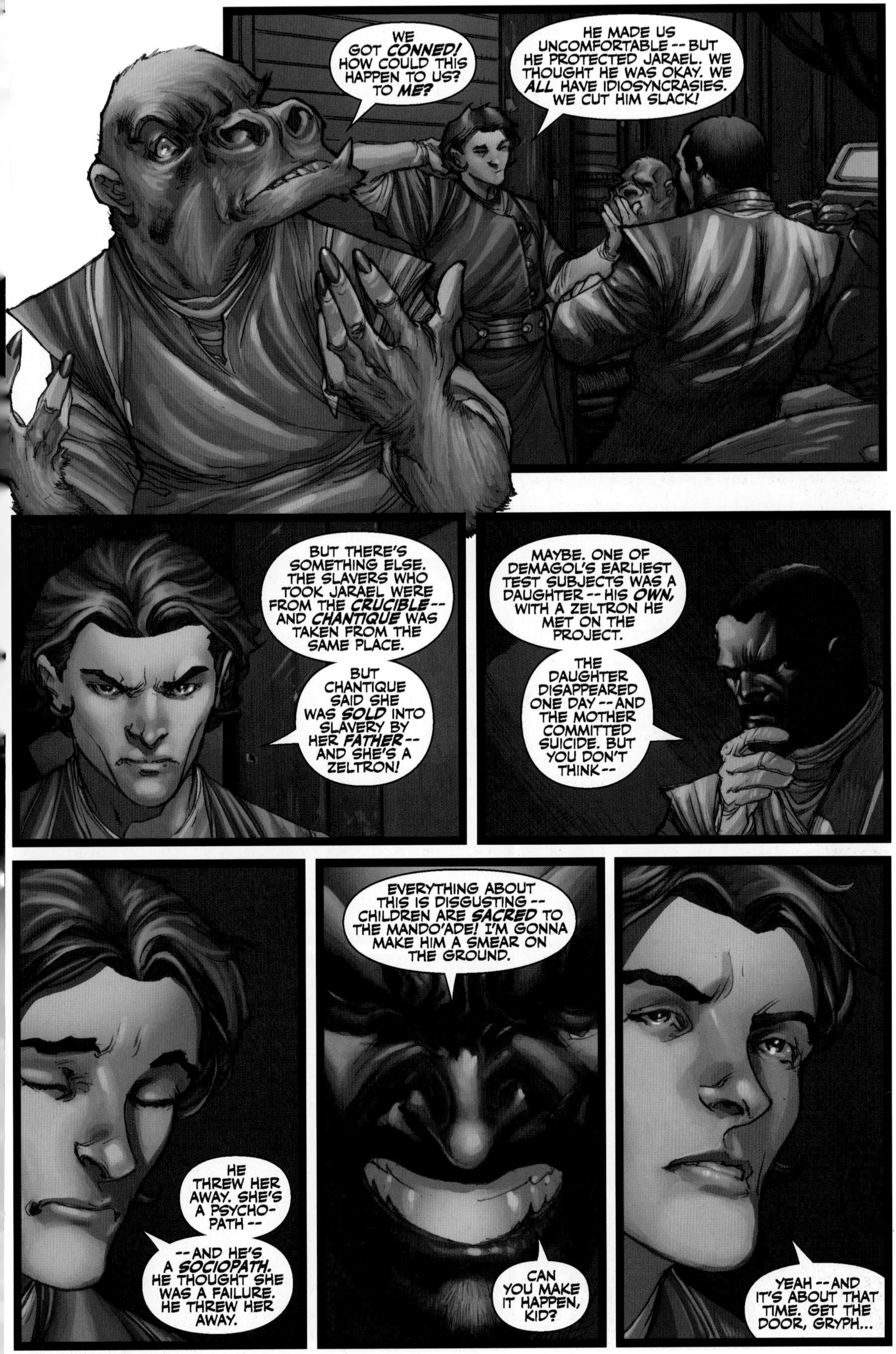
WE GOT *CONNED!* HOW COULD THIS HAPPEN TO US? TO *ME?*
HE MADE US UNCOMFORTABLE -- BUT HE PROTECTED JARAEL. WE THOUGHT HE WAS OKAY. WE *ALL* HAVE IDIOSYNCRASIES. WE CUT HIM SLACK!
BUT THERE'S SOMETHING ELSE. THE SLAVERS WHO TOOK JARAEL WERE FROM THE *CRUCIBLE* -- AND *CHANTIQUE* WAS TAKEN FROM THE SAME PLACE.
BUT CHANTIQUE SAID SHE WAS *SOLD* INTO SLAVERY BY HER *FATHER* -- AND SHE'S A ZELTRON!
MAYBE. ONE OF DEMAGOL'S EARLIEST TEST SUBJECTS WAS A DAUGHTER -- HIS *OWN,* WITH A ZELTRON HE MET ON THE PROJECT.
THE DAUGHTER DISAPPEARED ONE DAY -- AND THE MOTHER COMMITTED SUICIDE. BUT YOU DON'T THINK --
HE THREW HER AWAY. SHE'S A PSYCHO-PATH --
-- AND HE'S A *SOCIOPATH.* HE THOUGHT SHE WAS A FAILURE. HE THREW HER AWAY.
EVERYTHING ABOUT THIS IS DISGUSTING -- CHILDREN ARE *SACRED* TO THE MANDO'ADE! I'M GONNA MAKE HIM A SMEAR ON THE GROUND.
CAN YOU MAKE IT HAPPEN, KID?
YEAH -- AND IT'S ABOUT THAT TIME. GET THE DOOR, GRYPH...

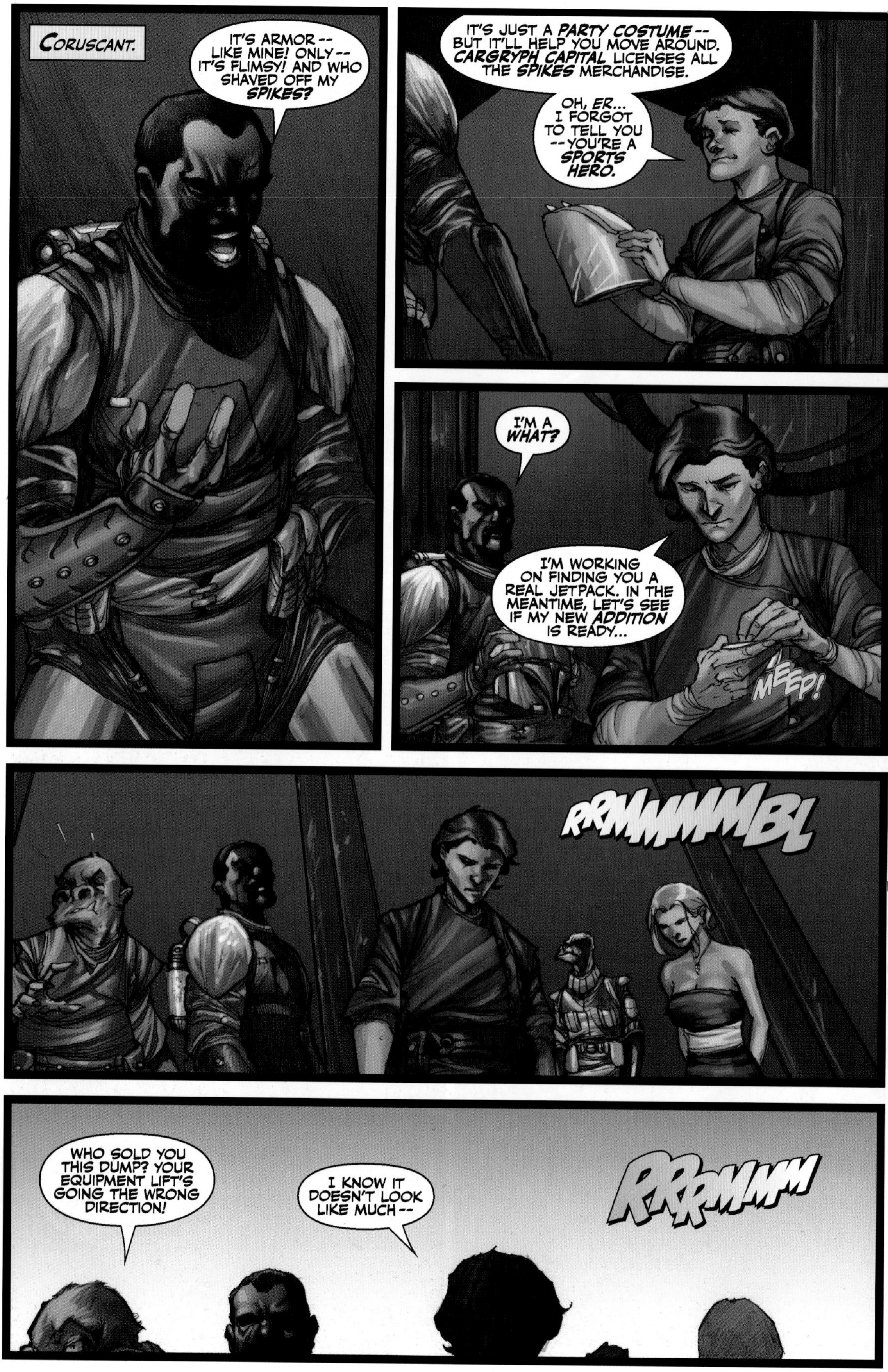
CORUSCANT.
IT'S ARMOR -- LIKE MINE! ONLY -- IT'S FLIMSY! AND WHO SHAVED OFF MY SPIKES?
IT'S JUST A PARTY COSTUME -- BUT IT'LL HELP YOU MOVE AROUND. CARGRYPH CAPITAL LICENSES ALL THE SPIKES MERCHANDISE.
OH, ER... I FORGOT TO TELL YOU -- YOU'RE A SPORTS HERO.
I'M A WHAT?
I'M WORKING ON FINDING YOU A REAL JETPACK. IN THE MEANTIME, LET'S SEE IF MY NEW ADDITION IS READY...
MEEP!
RRMMMMMBL
WHO SOLD YOU THIS DUMP? YOUR EQUIPMENT LIFT'S GOING THE WRONG DIRECTION!
I KNOW IT DOESN'T LOOK LIKE MUCH --
RRRMMMM

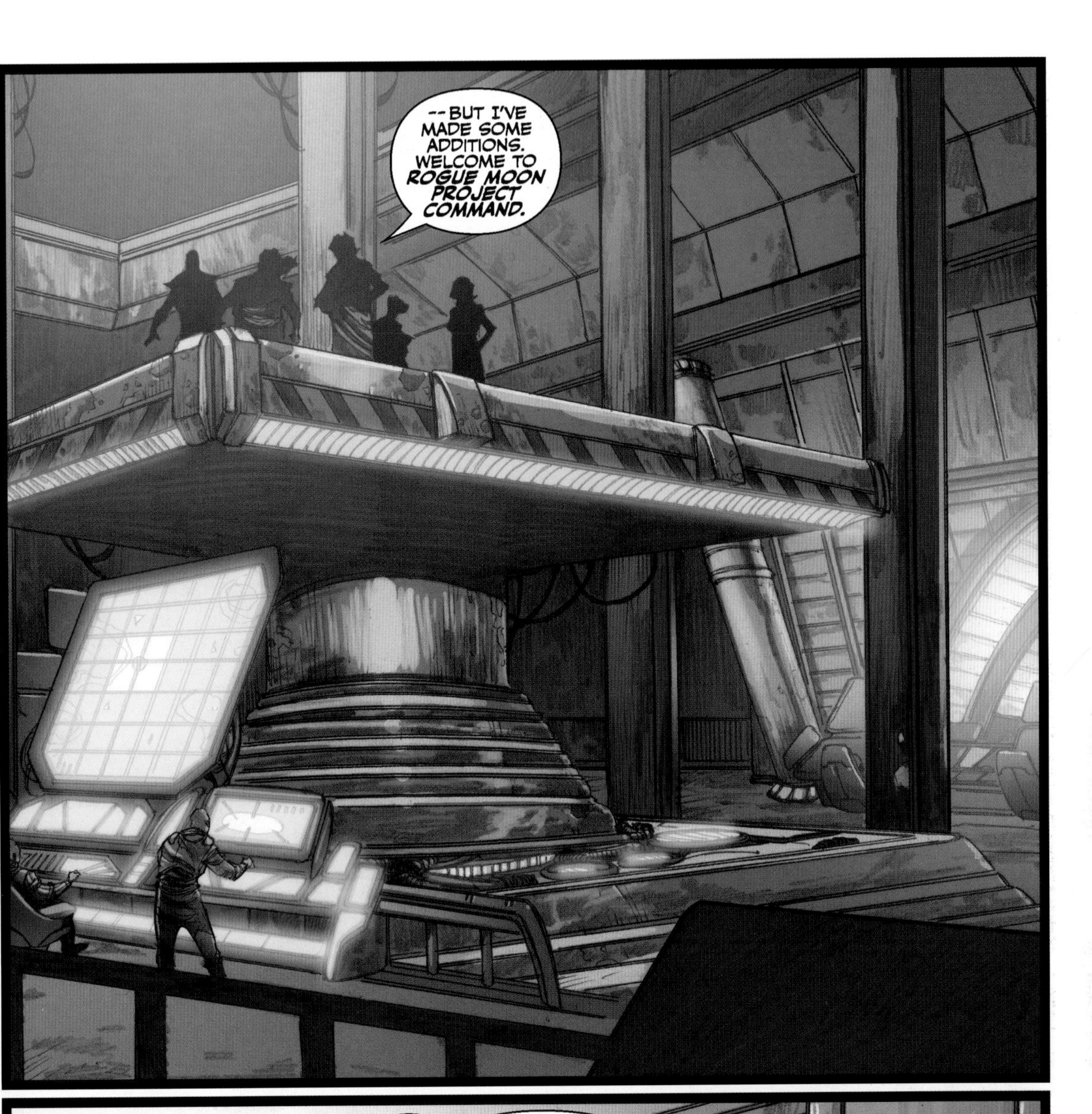
--BUT I'VE MADE SOME ADDITIONS. WELCOME TO ***ROGUE MOON PROJECT COMMAND.***

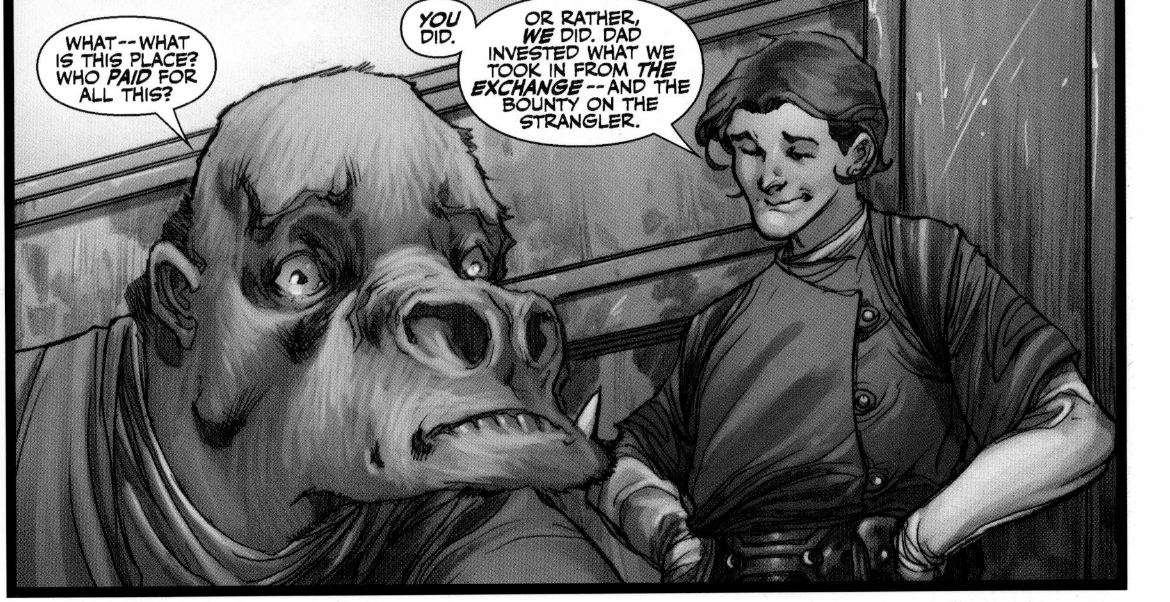
WHAT--WHAT IS THIS PLACE? WHO ***PAID*** FOR ALL THIS?
YOU DID.
OR RATHER, ***WE*** DID. DAD INVESTED WHAT WE TOOK IN FROM ***THE EXCHANGE***--AND THE BOUNTY ON THE STRANGLER.

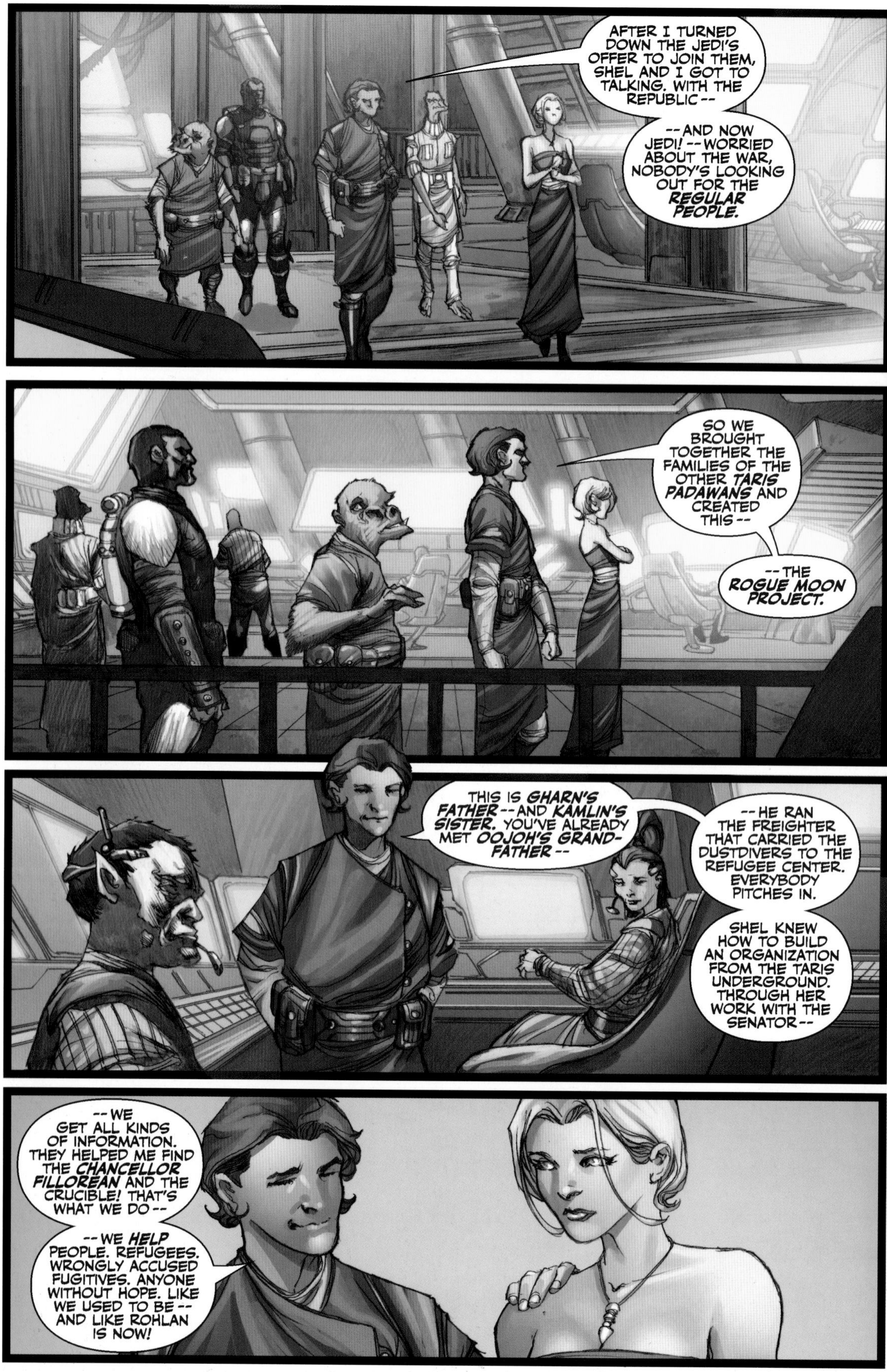
AFTER I TURNED DOWN THE JEDI'S OFFER TO JOIN THEM, SHEL AND I GOT TO TALKING. WITH THE REPUBLIC --
--AND NOW JEDI! --WORRIED ABOUT THE WAR, NOBODY'S LOOKING OUT FOR THE REGULAR PEOPLE.
SO WE BROUGHT TOGETHER THE FAMILIES OF THE OTHER TARIS PADAWANS AND CREATED THIS --
--THE ROGUE MOON PROJECT.
THIS IS GHARN'S FATHER --AND KAMLIN'S SISTER. YOU'VE ALREADY MET OOJOH'S GRAND-FATHER --
--HE RAN THE FREIGHTER THAT CARRIED THE DUSTDIVERS TO THE REFUGEE CENTER. EVERYBODY PITCHES IN.
SHEL KNEW HOW TO BUILD AN ORGANIZATION FROM THE TARIS UNDERGROUND. THROUGH HER WORK WITH THE SENATOR --
--WE GET ALL KINDS OF INFORMATION. THEY HELPED ME FIND THE CHANCELLOR FILLOREAN AND THE CRUCIBLE! THAT'S WHAT WE DO --
--WE HELP PEOPLE. REFUGEES. WRONGLY ACCUSED FUGITIVES. ANYONE WITHOUT HOPE. LIKE WE USED TO BE -- AND LIKE ROHLAN IS NOW!

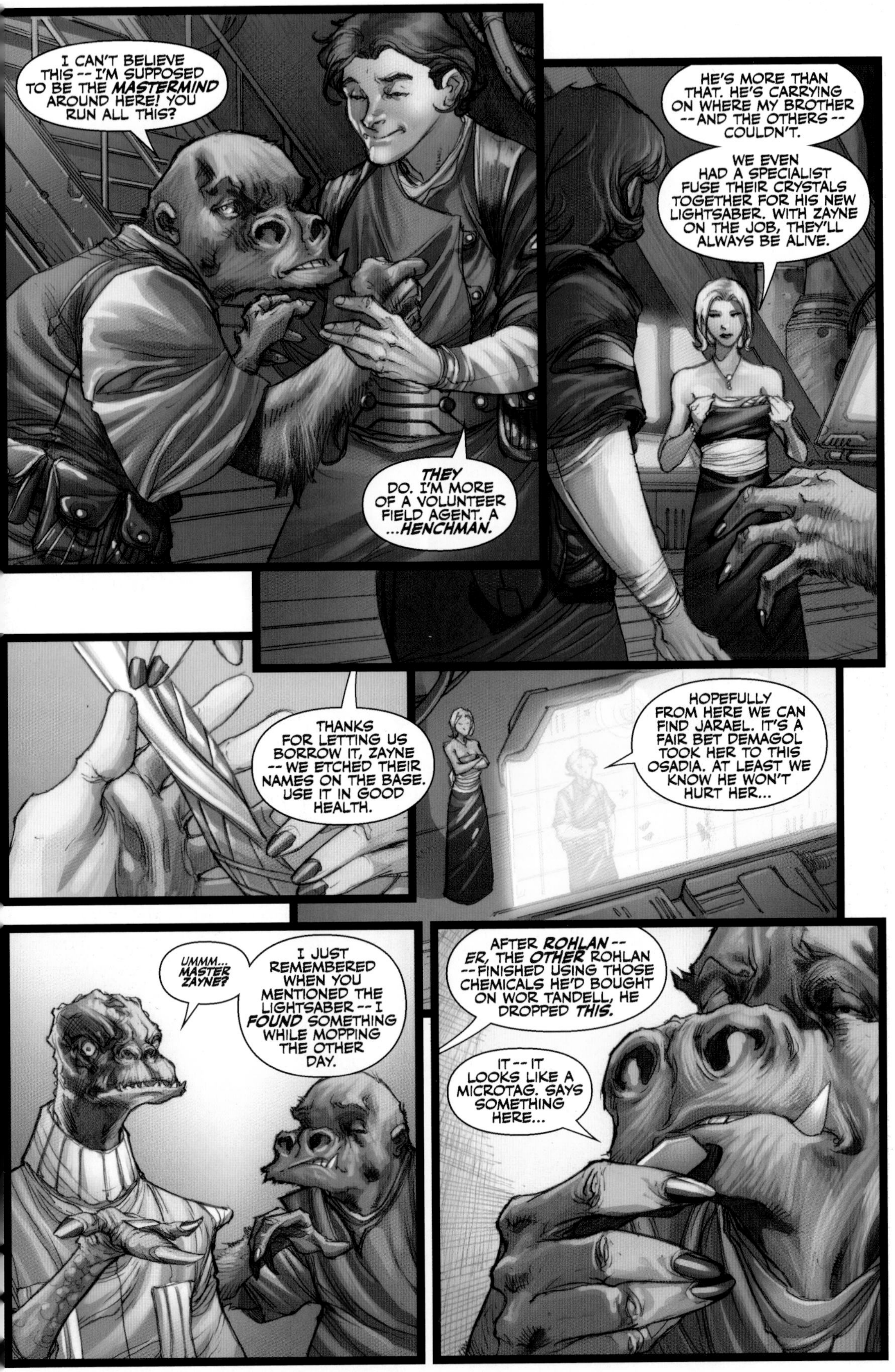
I CAN'T BELIEVE THIS -- I'M SUPPOSED TO BE THE *MASTERMIND* AROUND HERE! YOU RUN ALL THIS?
THEY DO. I'M MORE OF A VOLUNTEER FIELD AGENT. A ...*HENCHMAN.*
HE'S MORE THAN THAT. HE'S CARRYING ON WHERE MY BROTHER -- AND THE OTHERS -- COULDN'T.
WE EVEN HAD A SPECIALIST FUSE THEIR CRYSTALS TOGETHER FOR HIS NEW LIGHTSABER. WITH ZAYNE ON THE JOB, THEY'LL ALWAYS BE ALIVE.
THANKS FOR LETTING US BORROW IT, ZAYNE -- WE ETCHED THEIR NAMES ON THE BASE. USE IT IN GOOD HEALTH.
HOPEFULLY FROM HERE WE CAN FIND JARAEL. IT'S A FAIR BET DEMAGOL TOOK HER TO THIS OSADIA. AT LEAST WE KNOW HE WON'T HURT HER...
UMMM... MASTER ZAYNE?
I JUST REMEMBERED WHEN YOU MENTIONED THE LIGHTSABER -- I *FOUND* SOMETHING WHILE MOPPING THE OTHER DAY.
AFTER *ROHLAN* -- *ER,* THE *OTHER* ROHLAN -- FINISHED USING THOSE CHEMICALS HE'D BOUGHT ON WOR TANDELL, HE DROPPED *THIS.*
IT -- IT LOOKS LIKE A MICROTAG. SAYS SOMETHING HERE...

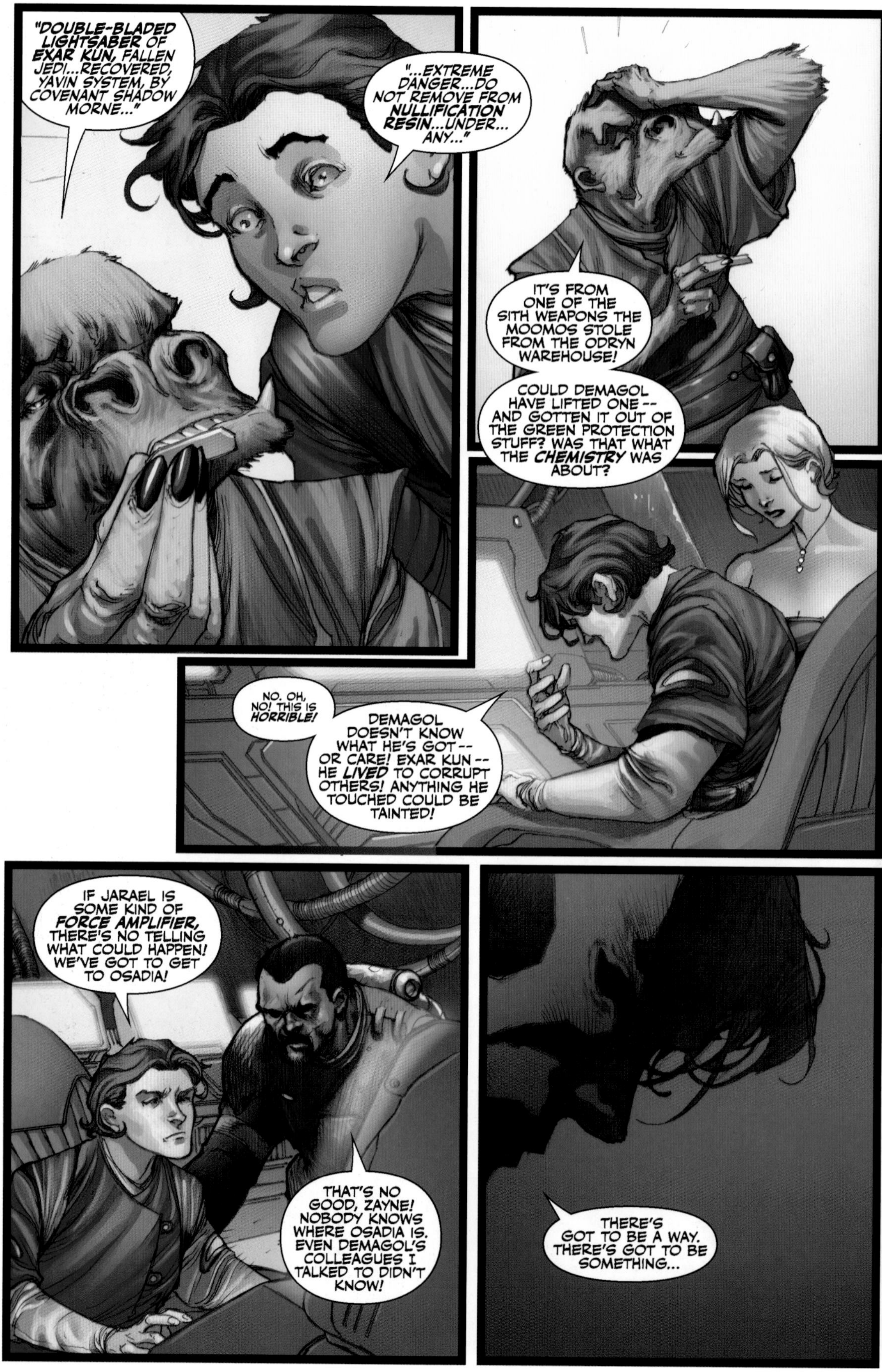
"DOUBLE-BLADED LIGHTSABER OF EXAR KUN, FALLEN JEDI...RECOVERED, YAVIN SYSTEM, BY COVENANT SHADOW MORNE..."
"...EXTREME DANGER...DO NOT REMOVE FROM NULLIFICATION RESIN...UNDER... ANY..."
IT'S FROM ONE OF THE SITH WEAPONS THE MOOMOS STOLE FROM THE ODRYN WAREHOUSE!
COULD DEMAGOL HAVE LIFTED ONE -- AND GOTTEN IT OUT OF THE GREEN PROTECTION STUFF? WAS THAT WHAT THE CHEMISTRY WAS ABOUT?
NO. OH, NO! THIS IS HORRIBLE!
DEMAGOL DOESN'T KNOW WHAT HE'S GOT -- OR CARE! EXAR KUN -- HE LIVED TO CORRUPT OTHERS! ANYTHING HE TOUCHED COULD BE TAINTED!
IF JARAEL IS SOME KIND OF FORCE AMPLIFIER, THERE'S NO TELLING WHAT COULD HAPPEN! WE'VE GOT TO GET TO OSADIA!
THAT'S NO GOOD, ZAYNE! NOBODY KNOWS WHERE OSADIA IS. EVEN DEMAGOL'S COLLEAGUES I TALKED TO DIDN'T KNOW!
THERE'S GOT TO BE A WAY. THERE'S GOT TO BE SOMETHING...

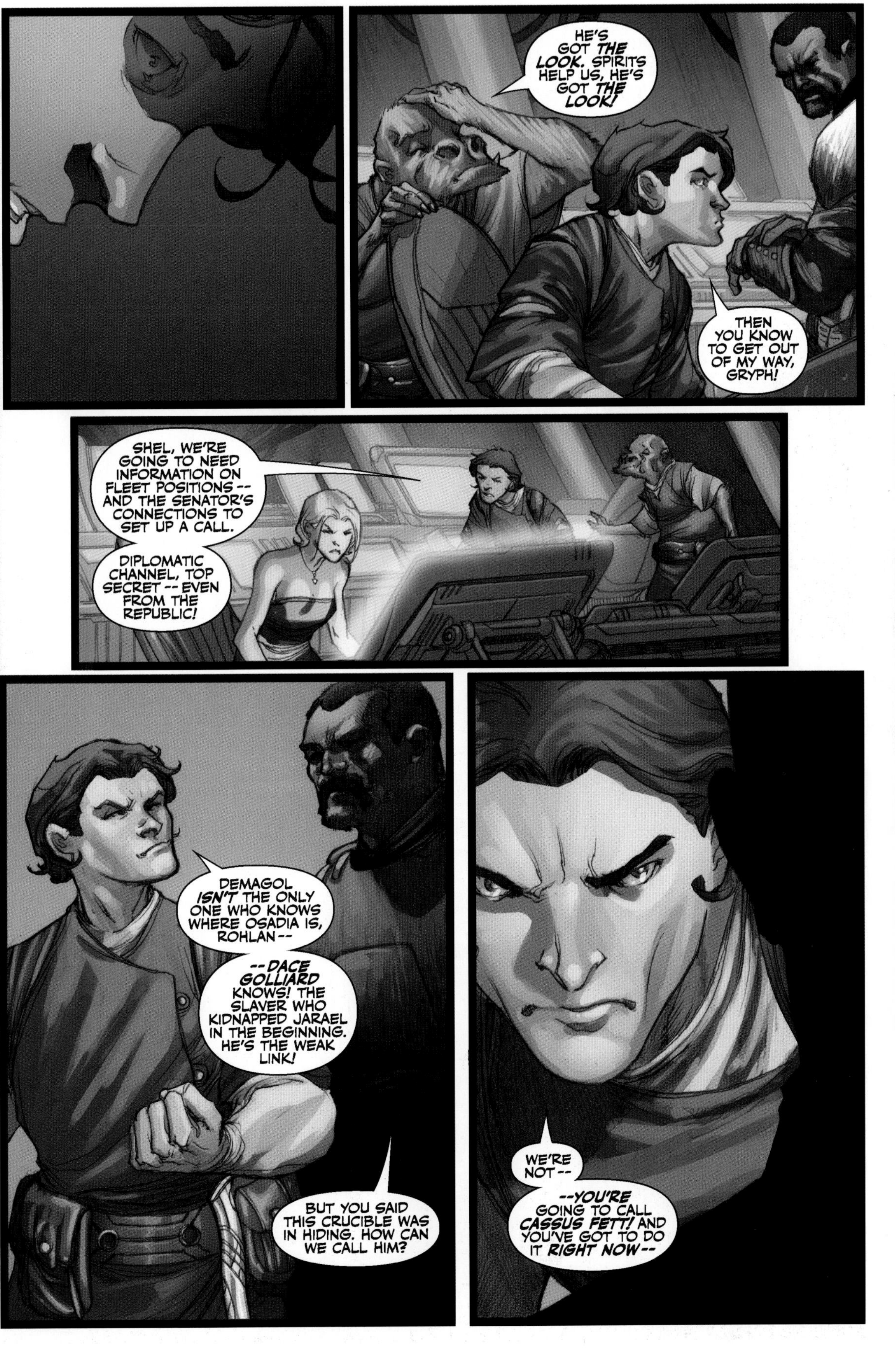
HE'S GOT THE LOOK. SPIRITS HELP US, HE'S GOT THE LOOK!
THEN YOU KNOW TO GET OUT OF MY WAY, GRYPH!
SHEL, WE'RE GOING TO NEED INFORMATION ON FLEET POSITIONS -- AND THE SENATOR'S CONNECTIONS TO SET UP A CALL.
DIPLOMATIC CHANNEL, TOP SECRET -- EVEN FROM THE REPUBLIC!
DEMAGOL ISN'T THE ONLY ONE WHO KNOWS WHERE OSADIA IS, ROHLAN--
--DACE GOLLIARD KNOWS! THE SLAVER WHO KIDNAPPED JARAEL IN THE BEGINNING. HE'S THE WEAK LINK!
BUT YOU SAID THIS CRUCIBLE WAS IN HIDING. HOW CAN WE CALL HIM?
WE'RE NOT--
--YOU'RE GOING TO CALL CASSUS FETT! AND YOU'VE GOT TO DO IT RIGHT NOW--

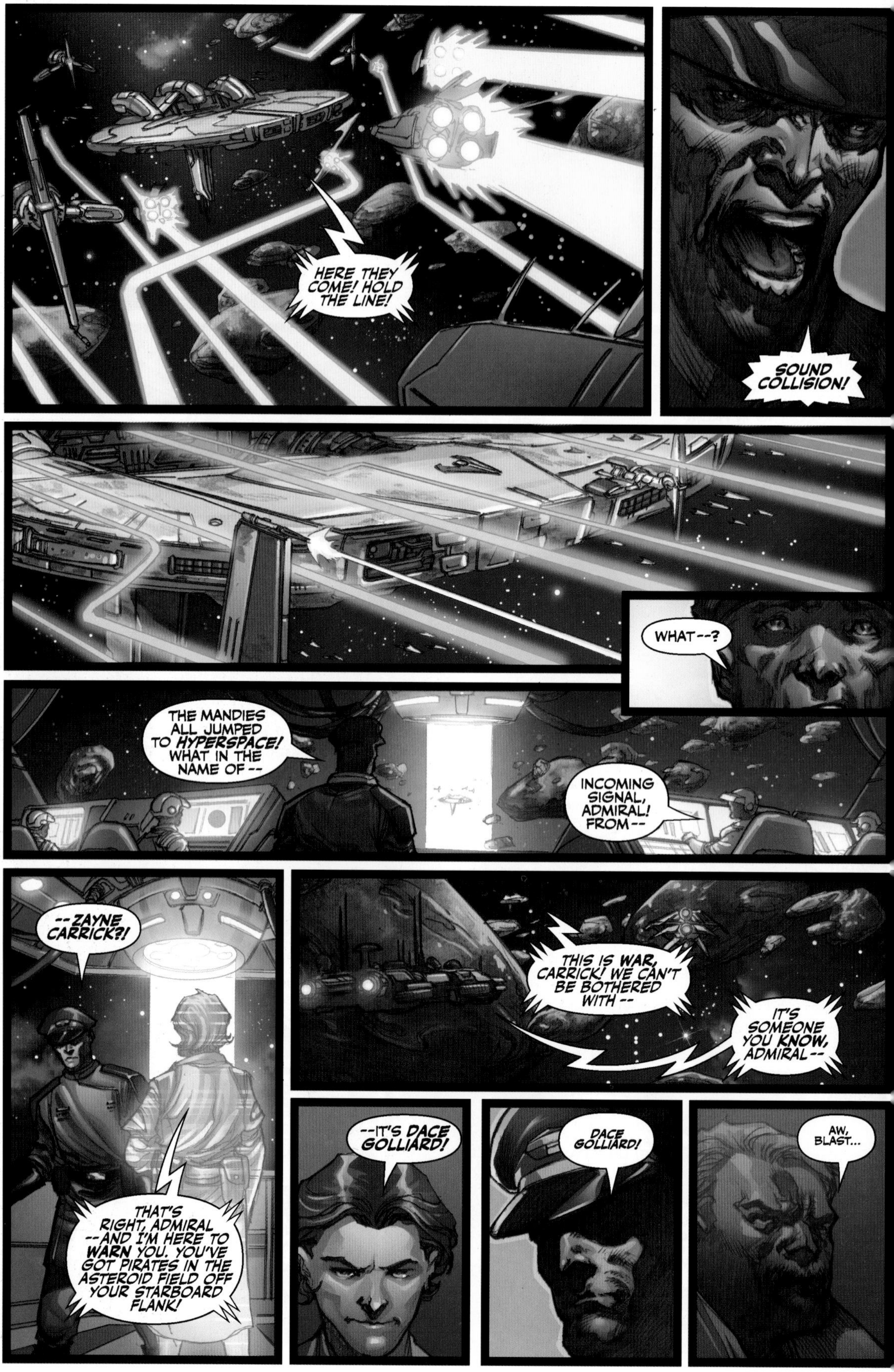
HERE THEY COME! HOLD THE LINE!
SOUND COLLISION!
WHAT--?
THE MANDIES ALL JUMPED TO *HYPERSPACE!* WHAT IN THE NAME OF --
INCOMING SIGNAL, ADMIRAL! FROM --
--ZAYNE CARRICK?!
THAT'S RIGHT, ADMIRAL --AND I'M HERE TO **WARN** YOU. YOU'VE GOT PIRATES IN THE ASTEROID FIELD OFF YOUR STARBOARD FLANK!
THIS IS *WAR,* CARRICK! WE CAN'T BE BOTHERED WITH --
IT'S SOMEONE YOU **KNOW,** ADMIRAL--
--IT'S *DACE GOLLIARD!*
DACE GOLLIARD!
AW, BLAST...

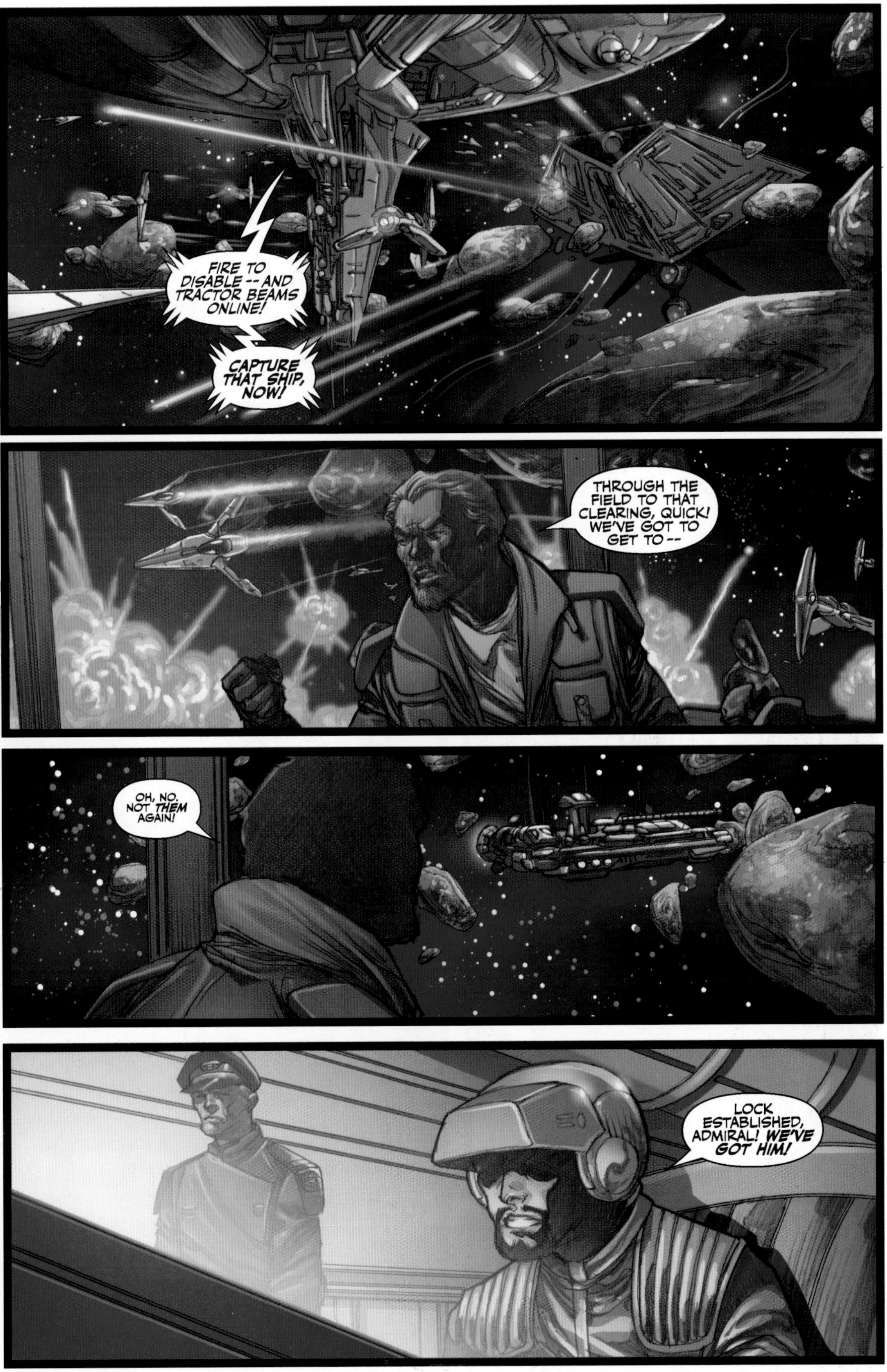
FIRE TO DISABLE -- AND TRACTOR BEAMS ONLINE!
CAPTURE THAT SHIP, NOW!
THROUGH THE FIELD TO THAT CLEARING, QUICK! WE'VE GOT TO GET TO --
OH, NO. NOT *THEM* AGAIN!
LOCK ESTABLISHED, ADMIRAL! *WE'VE GOT HIM!*

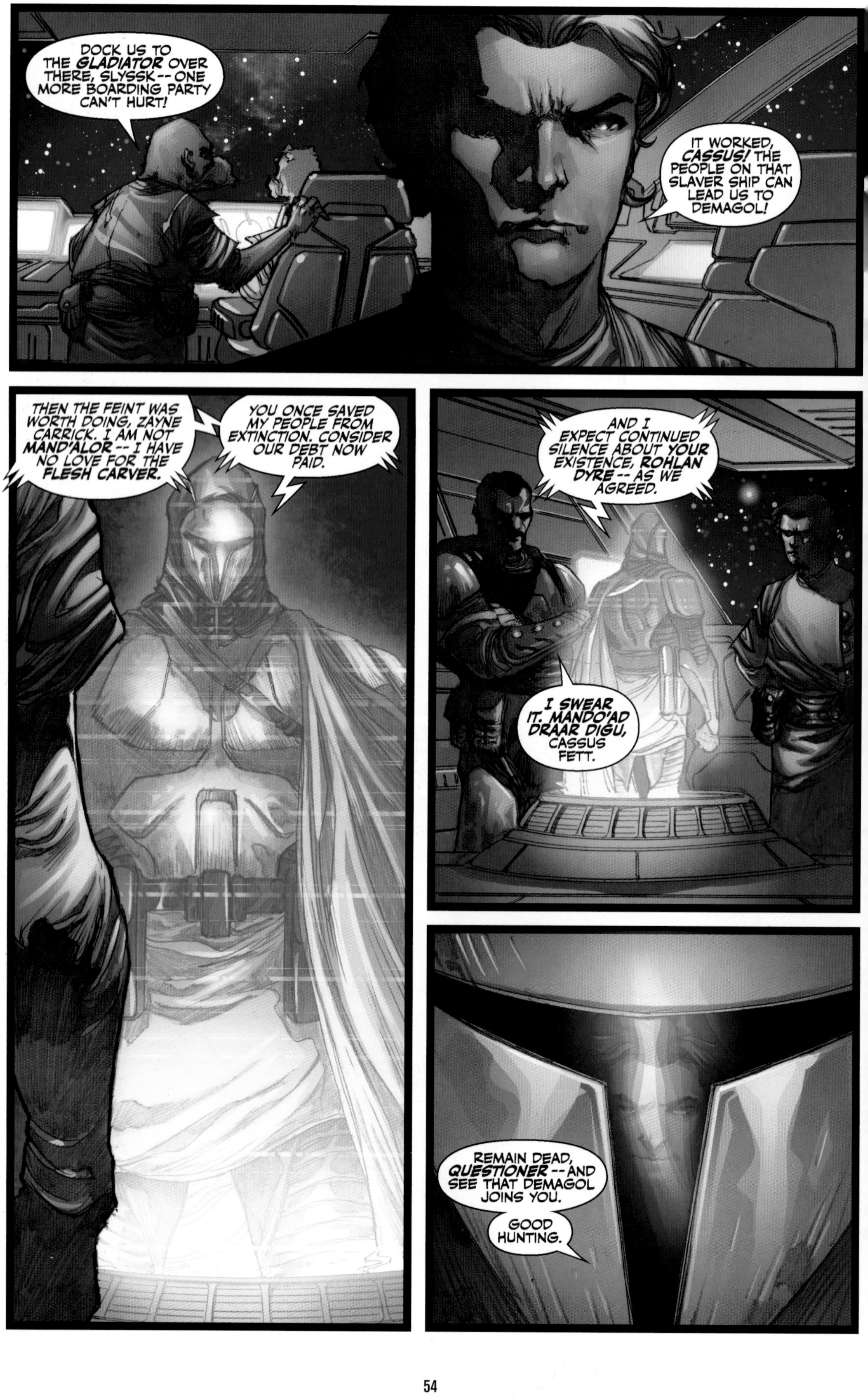
DOCK US TO THE GLADIATOR OVER THERE, SLYSSK -- ONE MORE BOARDING PARTY CAN'T HURT!
IT WORKED, CASSUS! THE PEOPLE ON THAT SLAVER SHIP CAN LEAD US TO DEMAGOL!
THEN THE FEINT WAS WORTH DOING, ZAYNE CARRICK. I AM NOT MAND'ALOR -- I HAVE NO LOVE FOR THE FLESH CARVER.
YOU ONCE SAVED MY PEOPLE FROM EXTINCTION. CONSIDER OUR DEBT NOW PAID.
AND I EXPECT CONTINUED SILENCE ABOUT YOUR EXISTENCE, ROHLAN DYRE -- AS WE AGREED.
I SWEAR IT. MANDO'AD DRAAR DIGU, CASSUS FETT.
REMAIN DEAD, QUESTIONER -- AND SEE THAT DEMAGOL JOINS YOU.
GOOD HUNTING.

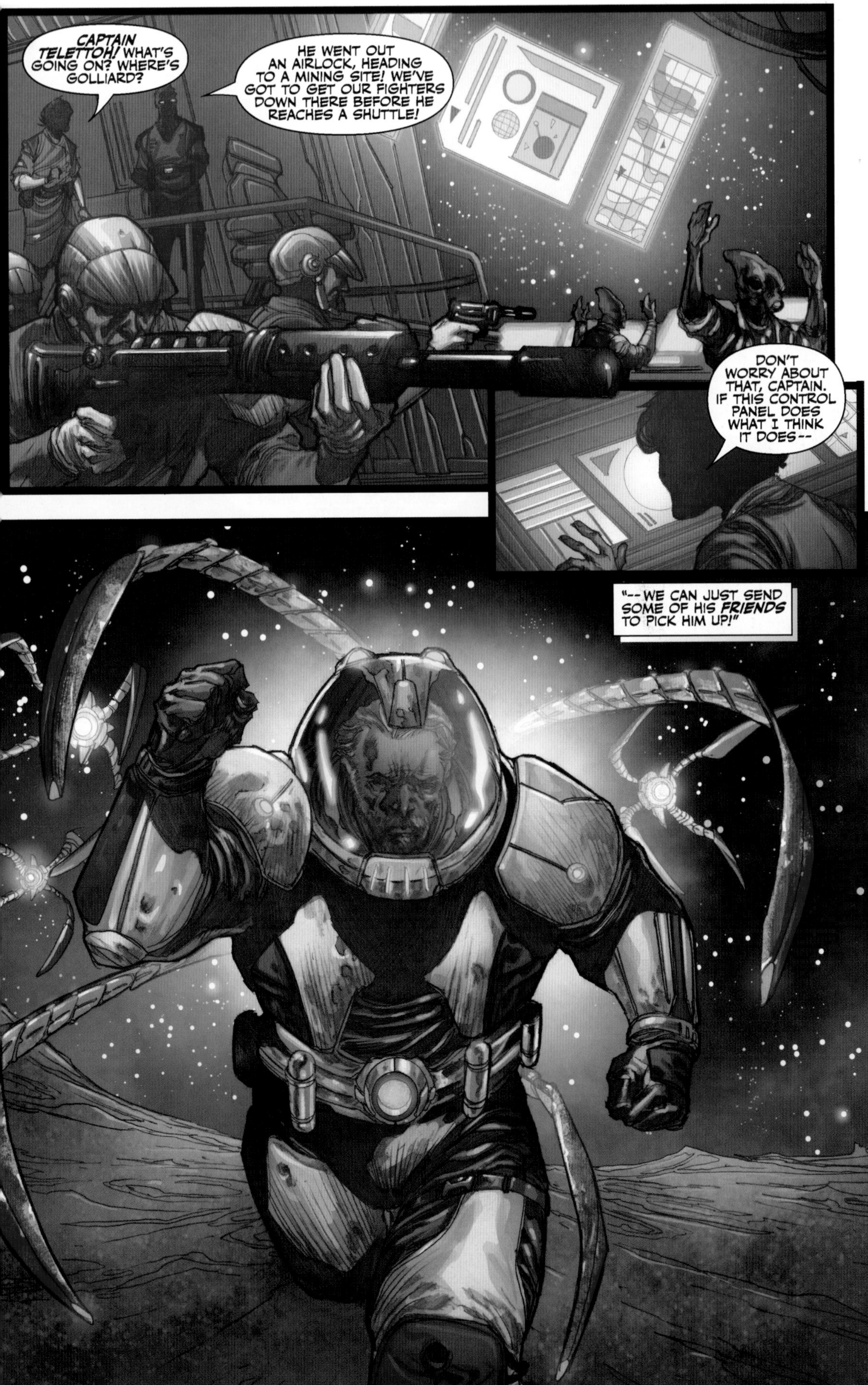
CAPTAIN TELETTOH! WHAT'S GOING ON? WHERE'S GOLLIARD?
HE WENT OUT AN AIRLOCK, HEADING TO A MINING SITE! WE'VE GOT TO GET OUR FIGHTERS DOWN THERE BEFORE HE REACHES A SHUTTLE!
DON'T WORRY ABOUT THAT, CAPTAIN. IF THIS CONTROL PANEL DOES WHAT I THINK IT DOES--
"--WE CAN JUST SEND SOME OF HIS FRIENDS TO PICK HIM UP!"

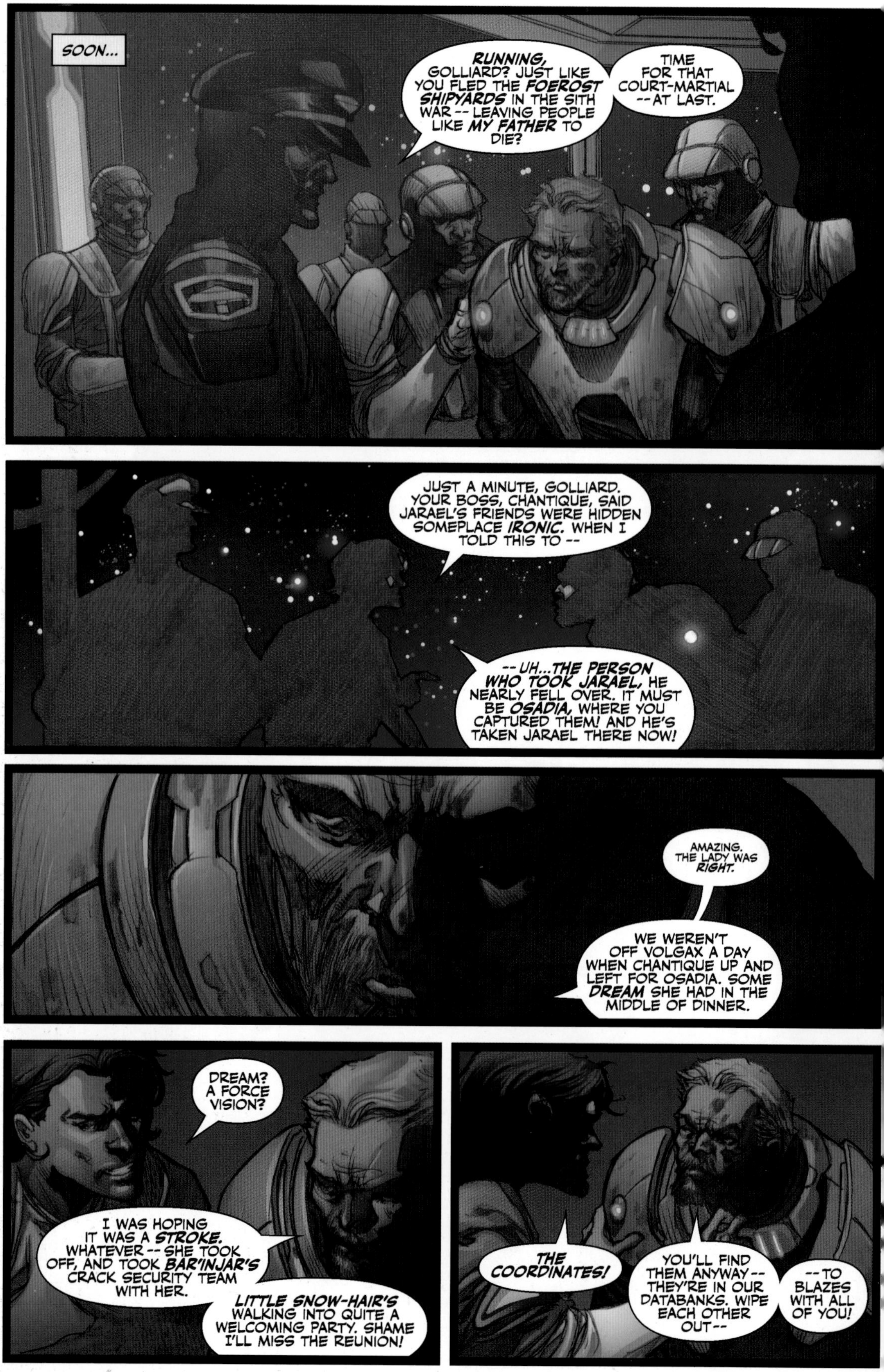
SOON...
RUNNING, GOLLIARD? JUST LIKE YOU FLED THE FOEROST SHIPYARDS IN THE SITH WAR -- LEAVING PEOPLE LIKE MY FATHER TO DIE?
TIME FOR THAT COURT-MARTIAL -- AT LAST.
JUST A MINUTE, GOLLIARD. YOUR BOSS, CHANTIQUE, SAID JARAEL'S FRIENDS WERE HIDDEN SOMEPLACE IRONIC. WHEN I TOLD THIS TO --
-- UH... THE PERSON WHO TOOK JARAEL, HE NEARLY FELL OVER. IT MUST BE OSADIA, WHERE YOU CAPTURED THEM! AND HE'S TAKEN JARAEL THERE NOW!
AMAZING. THE LADY WAS RIGHT.
WE WEREN'T OFF VOLGAX A DAY WHEN CHANTIQUE UP AND LEFT FOR OSADIA. SOME DREAM SHE HAD IN THE MIDDLE OF DINNER.
DREAM? A FORCE VISION?
I WAS HOPING IT WAS A STROKE. WHATEVER -- SHE TOOK OFF, AND TOOK BAR'INJAR'S CRACK SECURITY TEAM WITH HER.
LITTLE SNOW-HAIR'S WALKING INTO QUITE A WELCOMING PARTY. SHAME I'LL MISS THE REUNION!
THE COORDINATES!
YOU'LL FIND THEM ANYWAY -- THEY'RE IN OUR DATABANKS. WIPE EACH OTHER OUT--
-- TO BLAZES WITH ALL OF YOU!

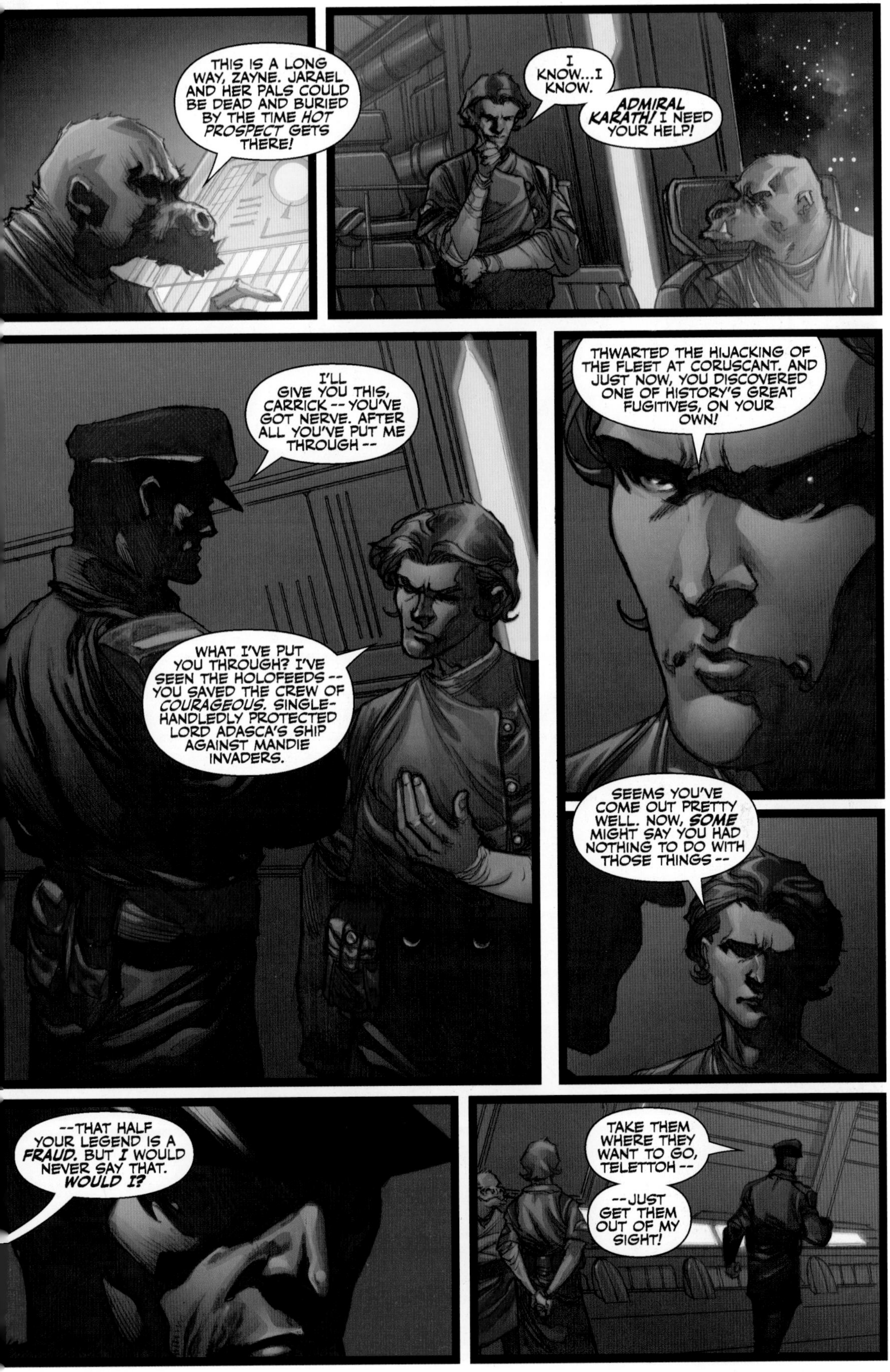
THIS IS A LONG WAY, ZAYNE. JARAEL AND HER PALS COULD BE DEAD AND BURIED BY THE TIME *HOT PROSPECT* GETS THERE!
I KNOW...I KNOW.
ADMIRAL KARATH! I NEED YOUR HELP!
I'LL GIVE YOU THIS, CARRICK -- YOU'VE GOT NERVE. AFTER ALL YOU'VE PUT ME THROUGH --
WHAT I'VE PUT YOU THROUGH? I'VE SEEN THE HOLOFEEDS -- YOU SAVED THE CREW OF *COURAGEOUS.* SINGLE-HANDLEDLY PROTECTED LORD ADASCA'S SHIP AGAINST MANDIE INVADERS.
THWARTED THE HIJACKING OF THE FLEET AT CORUSCANT. AND JUST NOW, YOU DISCOVERED ONE OF HISTORY'S GREAT FUGITIVES, ON YOUR OWN!
SEEMS YOU'VE COME OUT PRETTY WELL. NOW, *SOME* MIGHT SAY YOU HAD NOTHING TO DO WITH THOSE THINGS --
--THAT HALF YOUR LEGEND IS A *FRAUD.* BUT *I* WOULD NEVER SAY THAT. *WOULD I?*
TAKE THEM WHERE THEY WANT TO GO, TELETTOH --
--JUST GET THEM OUT OF MY SIGHT!

OSADIA -- OUTSIDE THE GROUNDS OF THE ABANDONED NEW GENERATION ACADEMY.

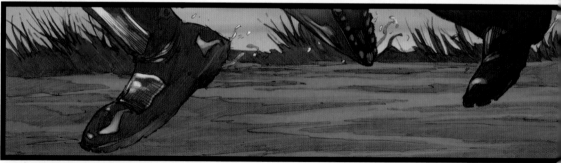

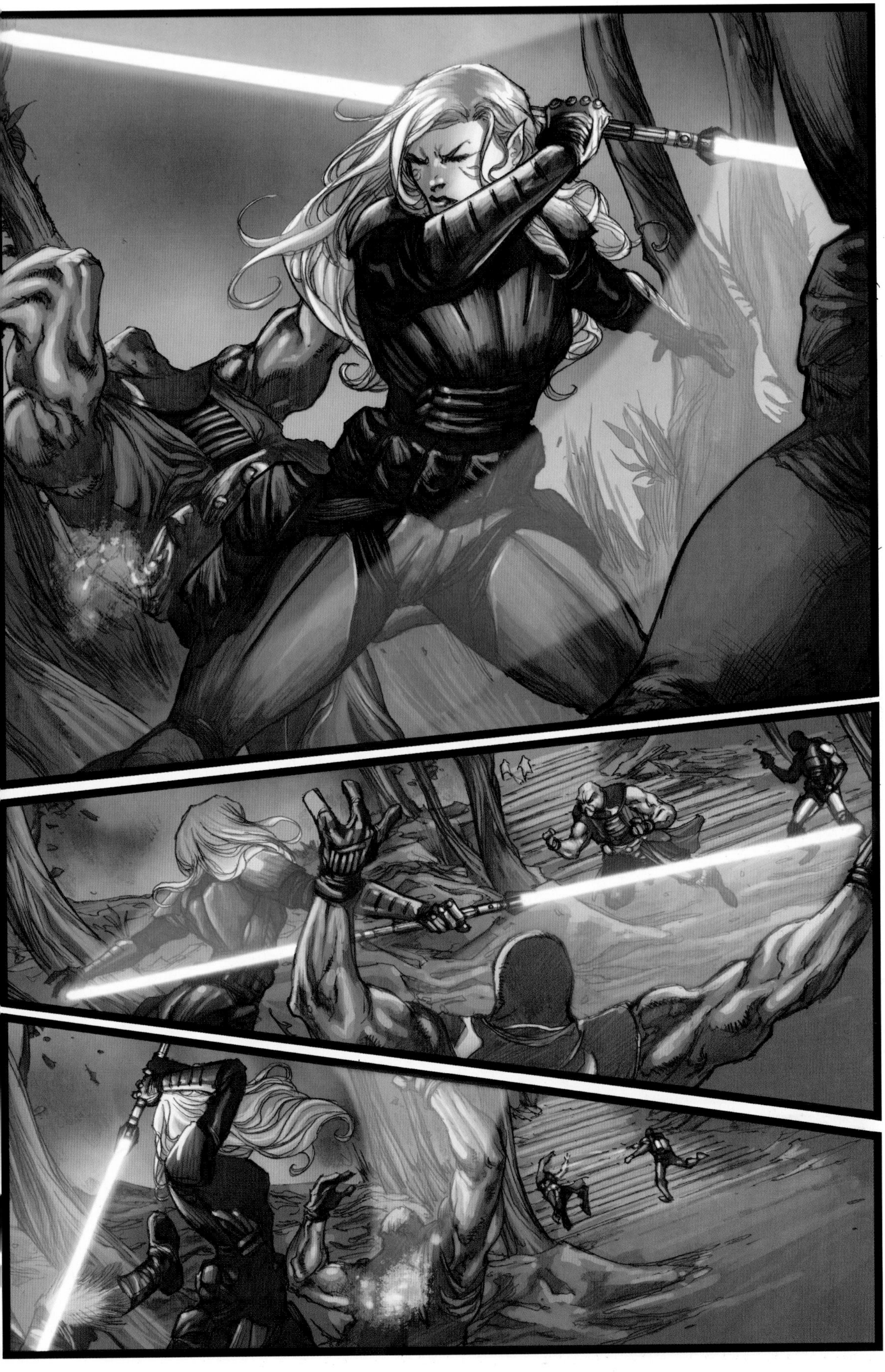

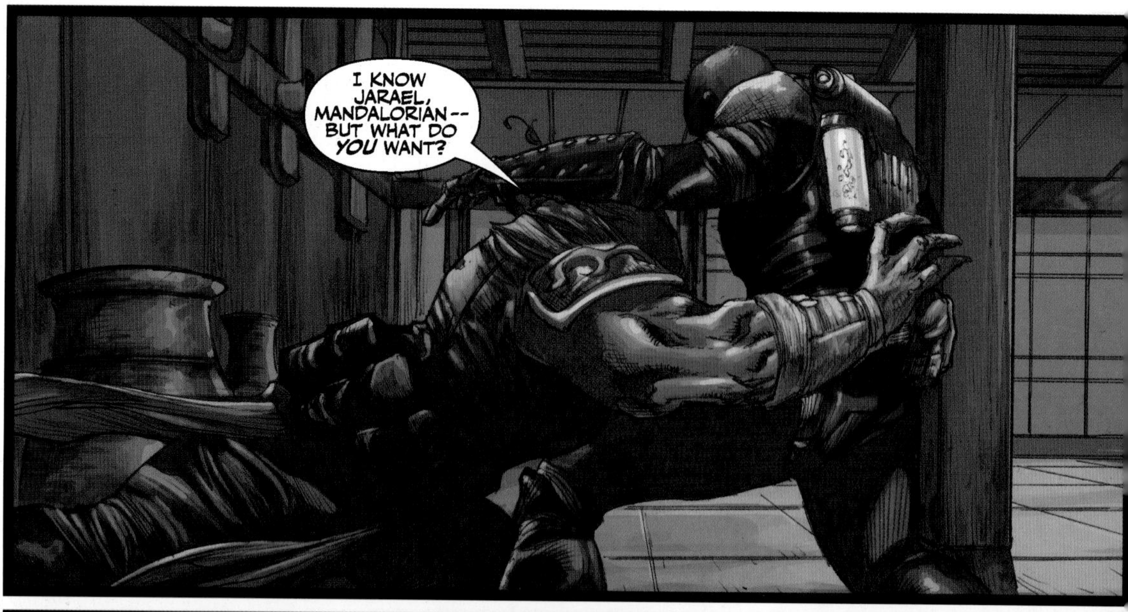
I KNOW JARAEL, MANDALORIAN-- BUT WHAT DO YOU WANT?

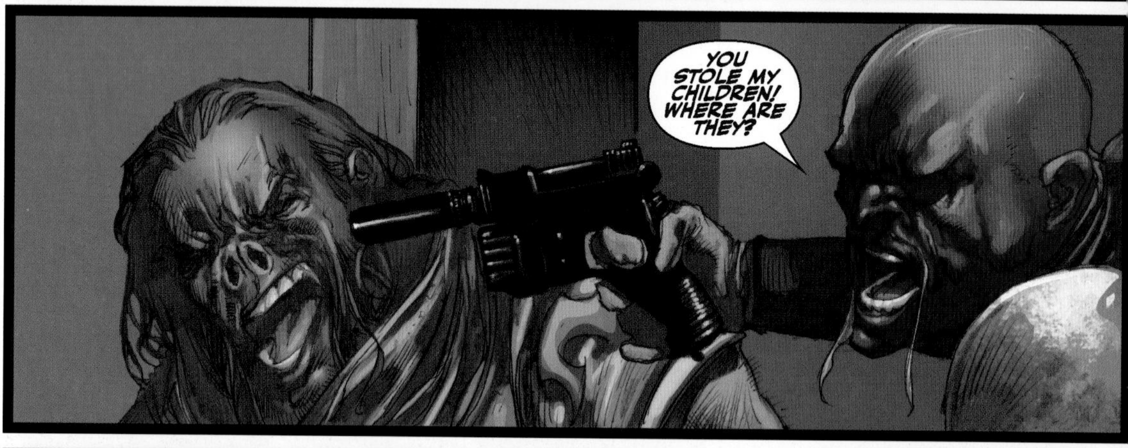
YOU STOLE MY CHILDREN! WHERE ARE THEY?

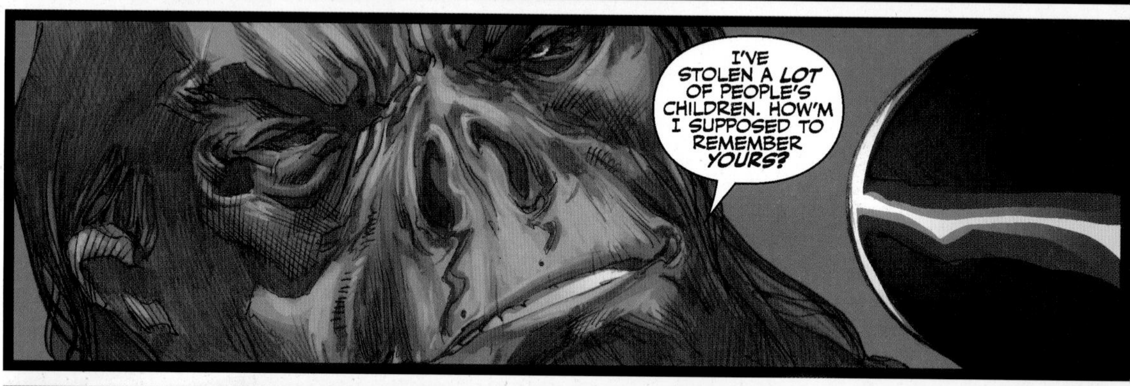
I'VE STOLEN A LOT OF PEOPLE'S CHILDREN. HOW'M I SUPPOSED TO REMEMBER YOURS?

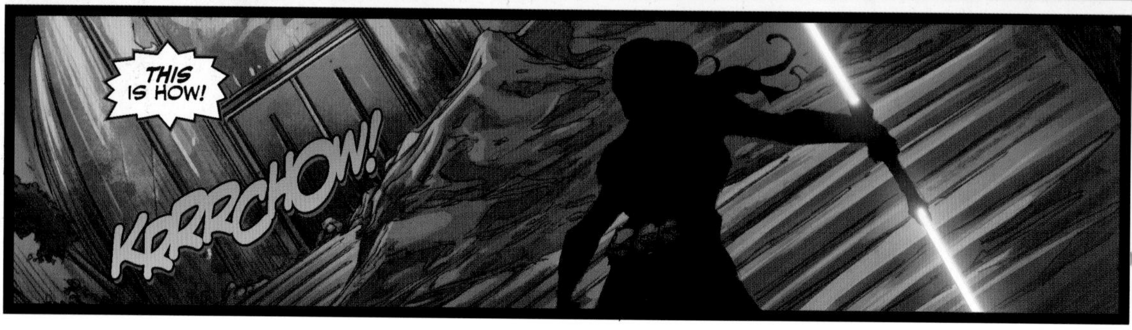
THIS IS HOW!
KRRRCHOW!

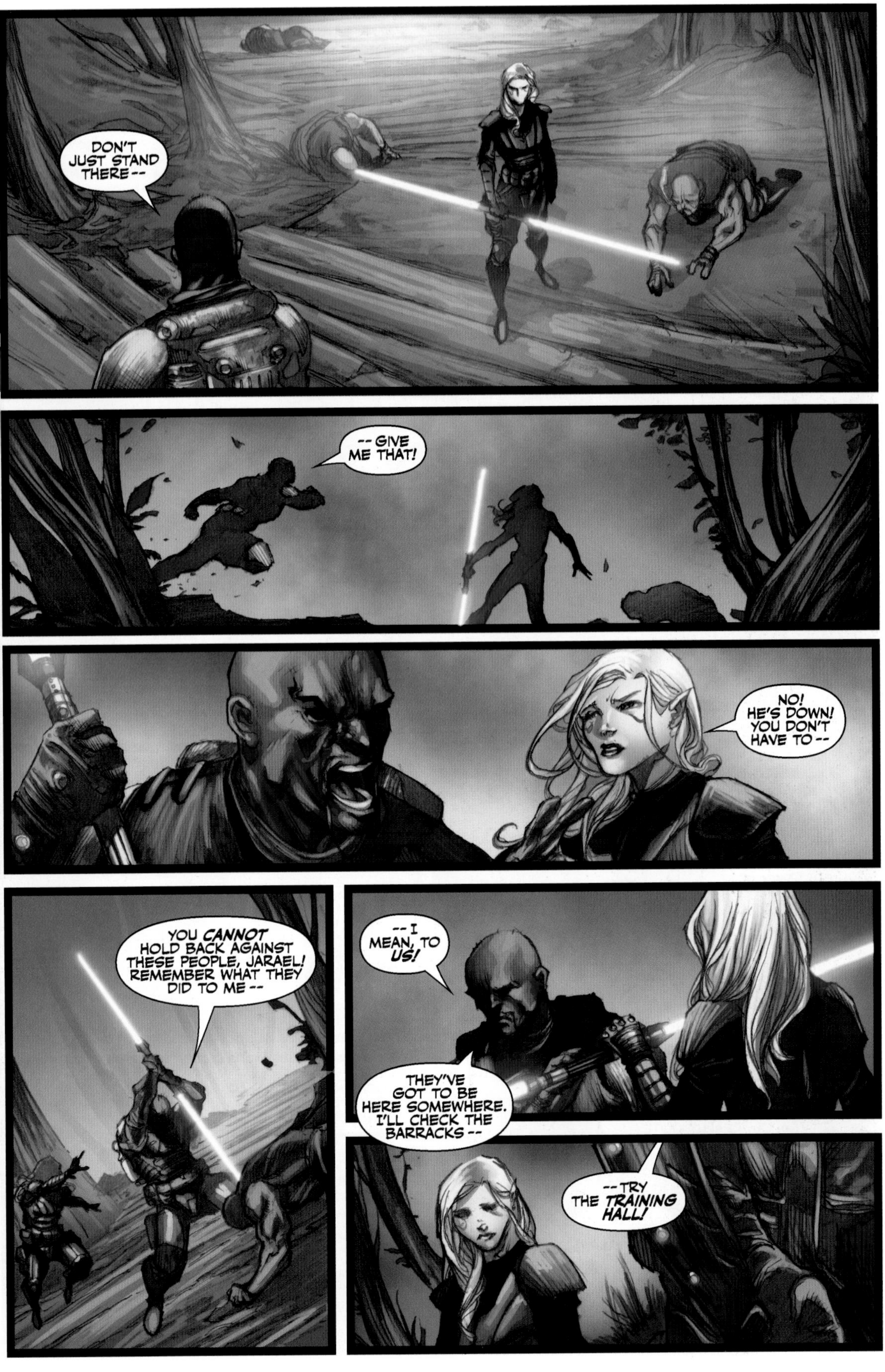
DON'T JUST STAND THERE--
--GIVE ME THAT!
NO! HE'S DOWN! YOU DON'T HAVE TO --
YOU *CANNOT* HOLD BACK AGAINST THESE PEOPLE, JARAEL! REMEMBER WHAT THEY DID TO ME --
--I MEAN, TO *US!*
THEY'VE GOT TO BE HERE SOMEWHERE. I'LL CHECK THE BARRACKS --
--TRY THE *TRAINING HALL!*

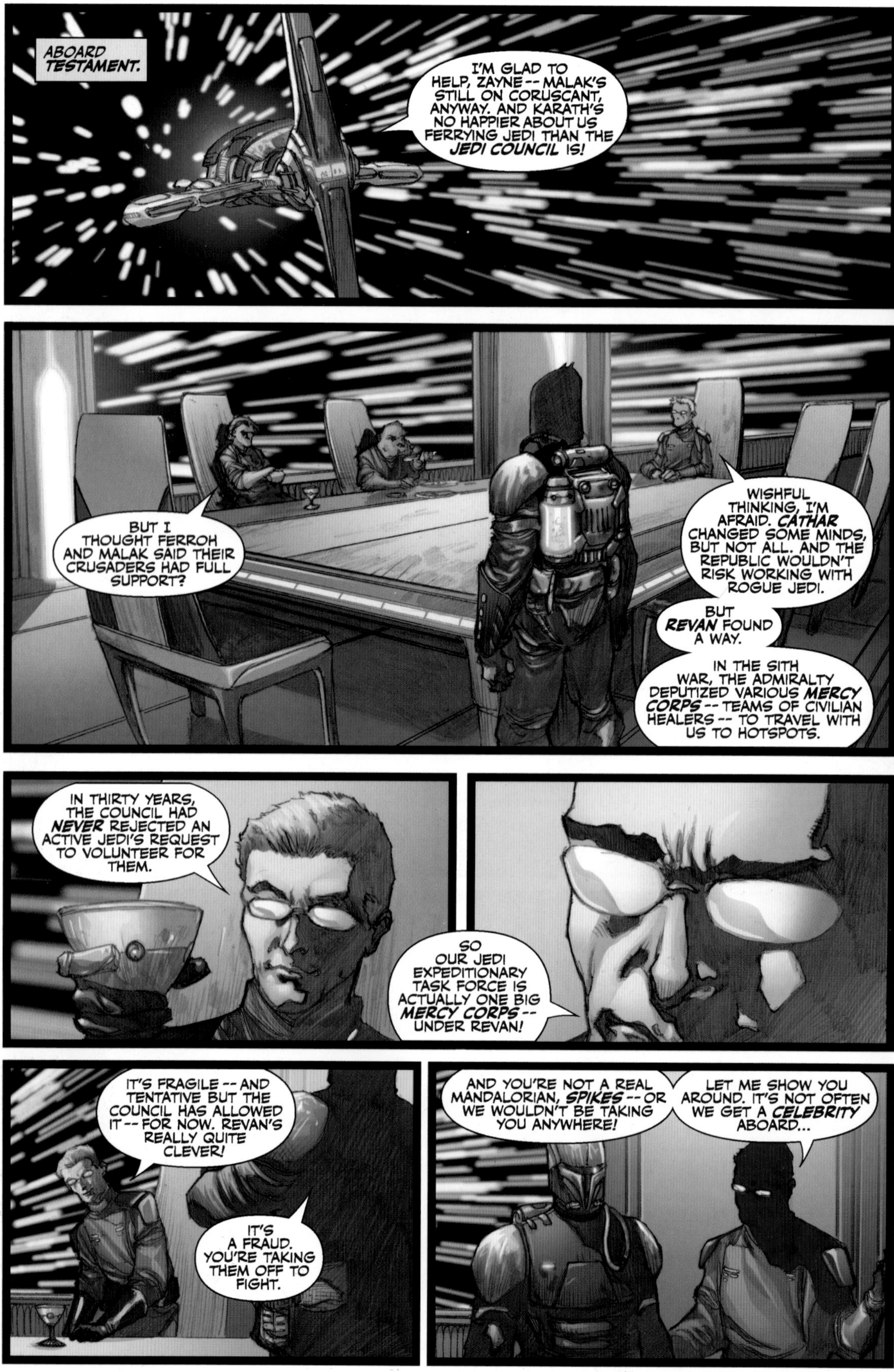
ABOARD TESTAMENT.
I'M GLAD TO HELP, ZAYNE -- MALAK'S STILL ON CORUSCANT, ANYWAY. AND KARATH'S NO HAPPIER ABOUT US FERRYING JEDI THAN THE JEDI COUNCIL IS!
BUT I THOUGHT FERROH AND MALAK SAID THEIR CRUSADERS HAD FULL SUPPORT?
WISHFUL THINKING, I'M AFRAID. CATHAR CHANGED SOME MINDS, BUT NOT ALL. AND THE REPUBLIC WOULDN'T RISK WORKING WITH ROGUE JEDI.
BUT REVAN FOUND A WAY.
IN THE SITH WAR, THE ADMIRALTY DEPUTIZED VARIOUS MERCY CORPS -- TEAMS OF CIVILIAN HEALERS -- TO TRAVEL WITH US TO HOTSPOTS.
IN THIRTY YEARS, THE COUNCIL HAD NEVER REJECTED AN ACTIVE JEDI'S REQUEST TO VOLUNTEER FOR THEM.
SO OUR JEDI EXPEDITIONARY TASK FORCE IS ACTUALLY ONE BIG MERCY CORPS -- UNDER REVAN!
IT'S FRAGILE -- AND TENTATIVE BUT THE COUNCIL HAS ALLOWED IT -- FOR NOW. REVAN'S REALLY QUITE CLEVER!
IT'S A FRAUD. YOU'RE TAKING THEM OFF TO FIGHT.
AND YOU'RE NOT A REAL MANDALORIAN, SPIKES -- OR WE WOULDN'T BE TAKING YOU ANYWHERE!
LET ME SHOW YOU AROUND. IT'S NOT OFTEN WE GET A CELEBRITY ABOARD...

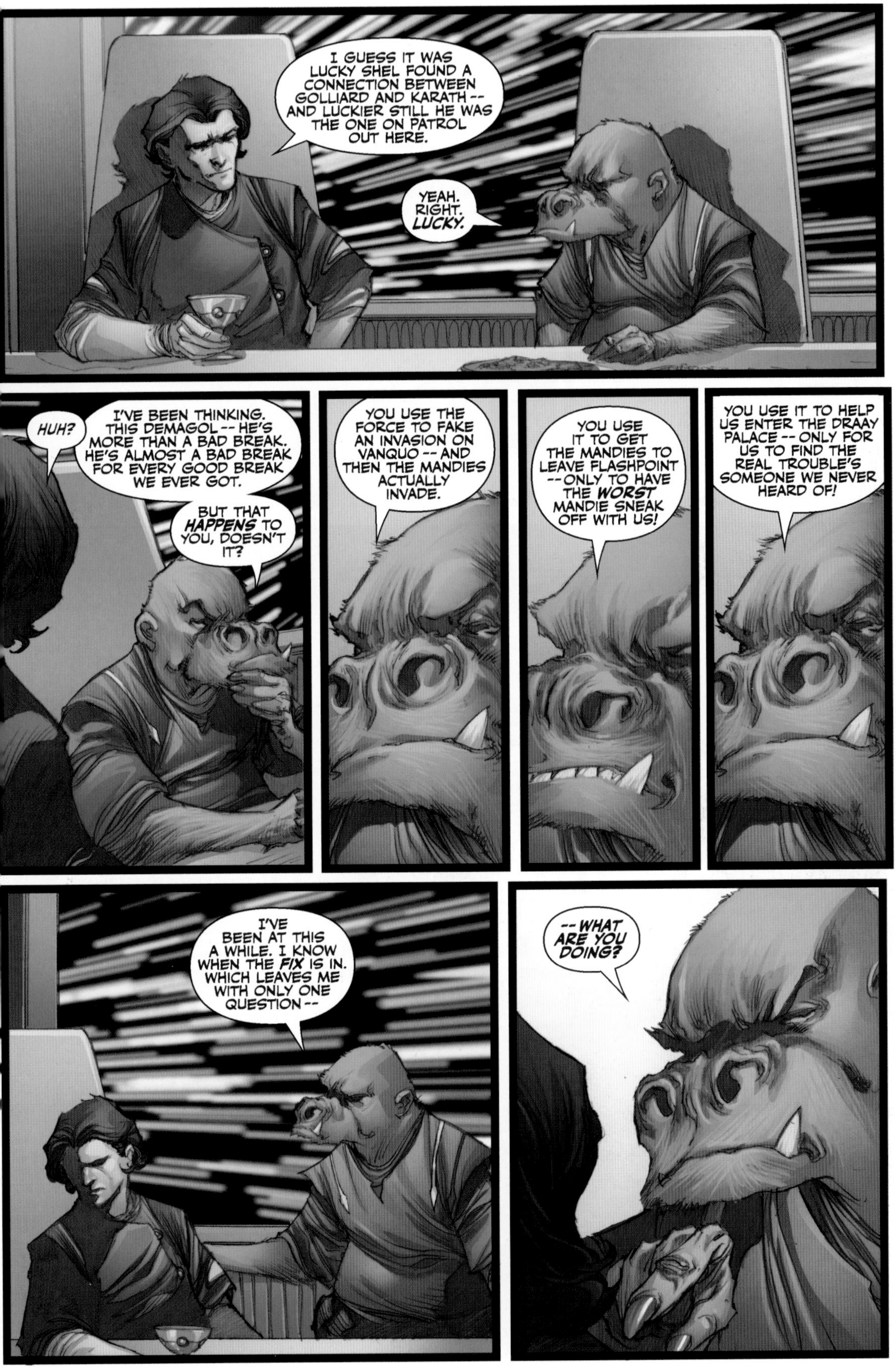
I GUESS IT WAS LUCKY SHEL FOUND A CONNECTION BETWEEN GOLLIARD AND KARATH -- AND LUCKIER STILL HE WAS THE ONE ON PATROL OUT HERE.
YEAH. RIGHT. LUCKY.
HUH?
I'VE BEEN THINKING. THIS DEMAGOL -- HE'S MORE THAN A BAD BREAK. HE'S ALMOST A BAD BREAK FOR EVERY GOOD BREAK WE EVER GOT.
BUT THAT HAPPENS TO YOU, DOESN'T IT?
YOU USE THE FORCE TO FAKE AN INVASION ON VANQUO -- AND THEN THE MANDIES ACTUALLY INVADE.
YOU USE IT TO GET THE MANDIES TO LEAVE FLASHPOINT -- ONLY TO HAVE THE WORST MANDIE SNEAK OFF WITH US!
YOU USE IT TO HELP US ENTER THE DRAAY PALACE -- ONLY FOR US TO FIND THE REAL TROUBLE'S SOMEONE WE NEVER HEARD OF!
I'VE BEEN AT THIS A WHILE. I KNOW WHEN THE FIX IS IN. WHICH LEAVES ME WITH ONLY ONE QUESTION --
-- WHAT ARE YOU DOING?

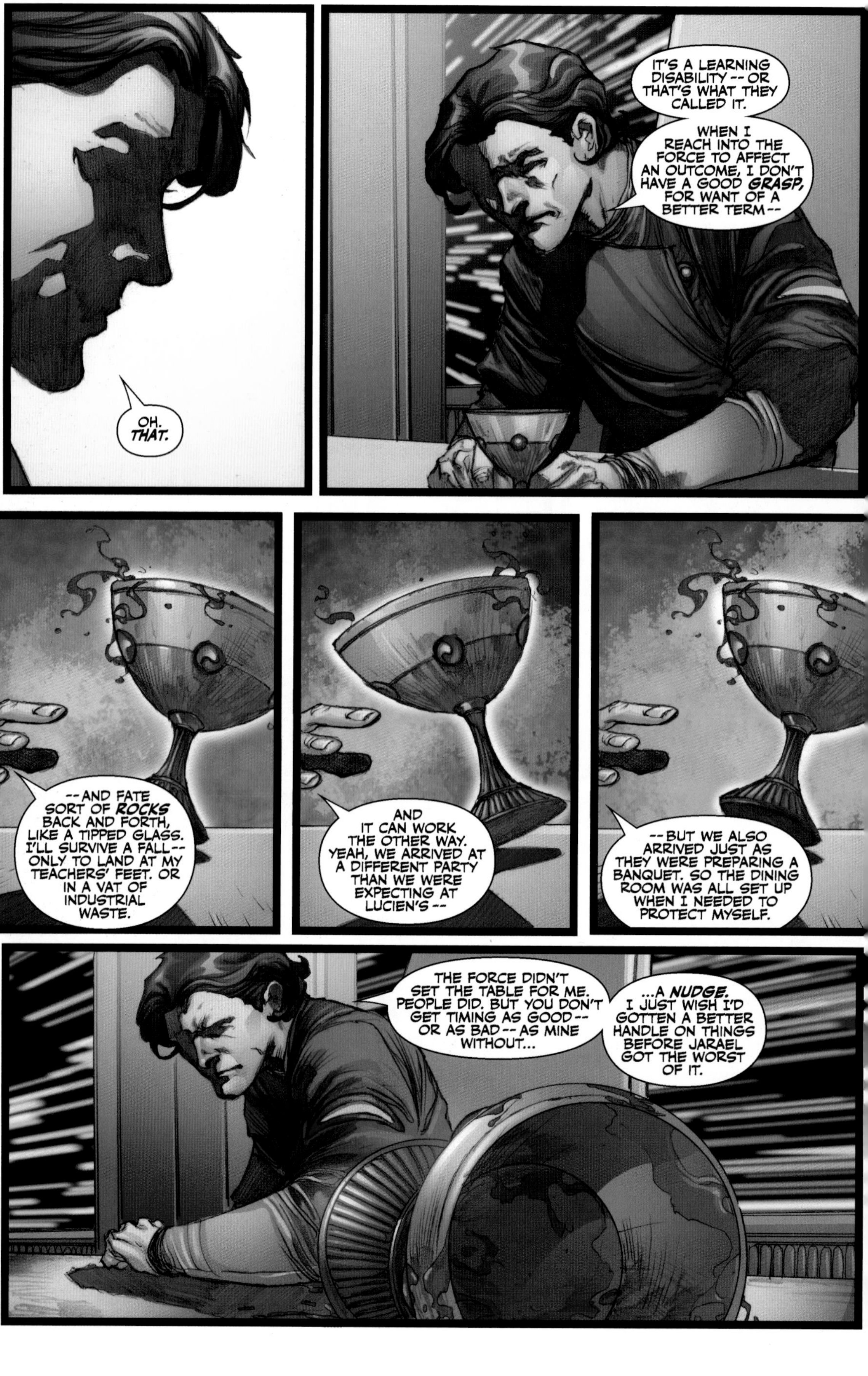
OH. *THAT.*
IT'S A LEARNING DISABILITY -- OR THAT'S WHAT THEY CALLED IT.
WHEN I REACH INTO THE FORCE TO AFFECT AN OUTCOME, I DON'T HAVE A GOOD *GRASP,* FOR WANT OF A BETTER TERM --
-- AND FATE SORT OF *ROCKS* BACK AND FORTH, LIKE A TIPPED GLASS. I'LL SURVIVE A FALL -- ONLY TO LAND AT MY TEACHERS' FEET. OR IN A VAT OF INDUSTRIAL WASTE.
AND IT CAN WORK THE OTHER WAY. YEAH, WE ARRIVED AT A DIFFERENT PARTY THAN WE WERE EXPECTING AT LUCIEN'S --
-- BUT WE ALSO ARRIVED JUST AS THEY WERE PREPARING A BANQUET. SO THE DINING ROOM WAS ALL SET UP WHEN I NEEDED TO PROTECT MYSELF.
THE FORCE DIDN'T SET THE TABLE FOR ME. PEOPLE DID. BUT YOU DON'T GET TIMING AS GOOD -- OR AS BAD -- AS MINE WITHOUT...
...A *NUDGE.* I JUST WISH I'D GOTTEN A BETTER HANDLE ON THINGS BEFORE JARAEL GOT THE WORST OF IT.

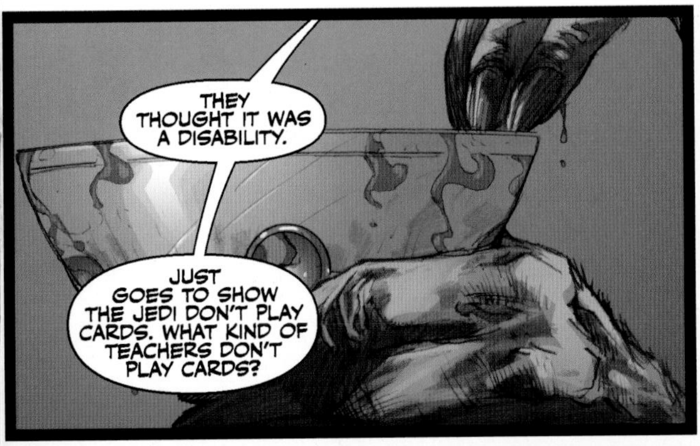
THEY THOUGHT IT WAS A DISABILITY.
JUST GOES TO SHOW THE JEDI DON'T PLAY CARDS. WHAT KIND OF TEACHERS DON'T PLAY CARDS?

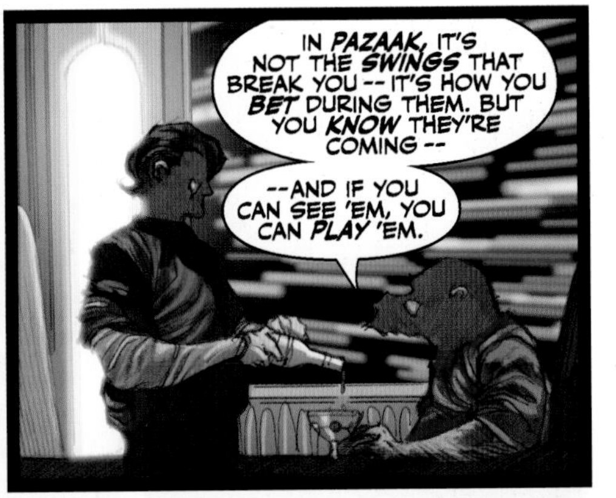
IN PAZAAK, IT'S NOT THE SWINGS THAT BREAK YOU -- IT'S HOW YOU BET DURING THEM. BUT YOU KNOW THEY'RE COMING --
--AND IF YOU CAN SEE 'EM, YOU CAN PLAY 'EM.

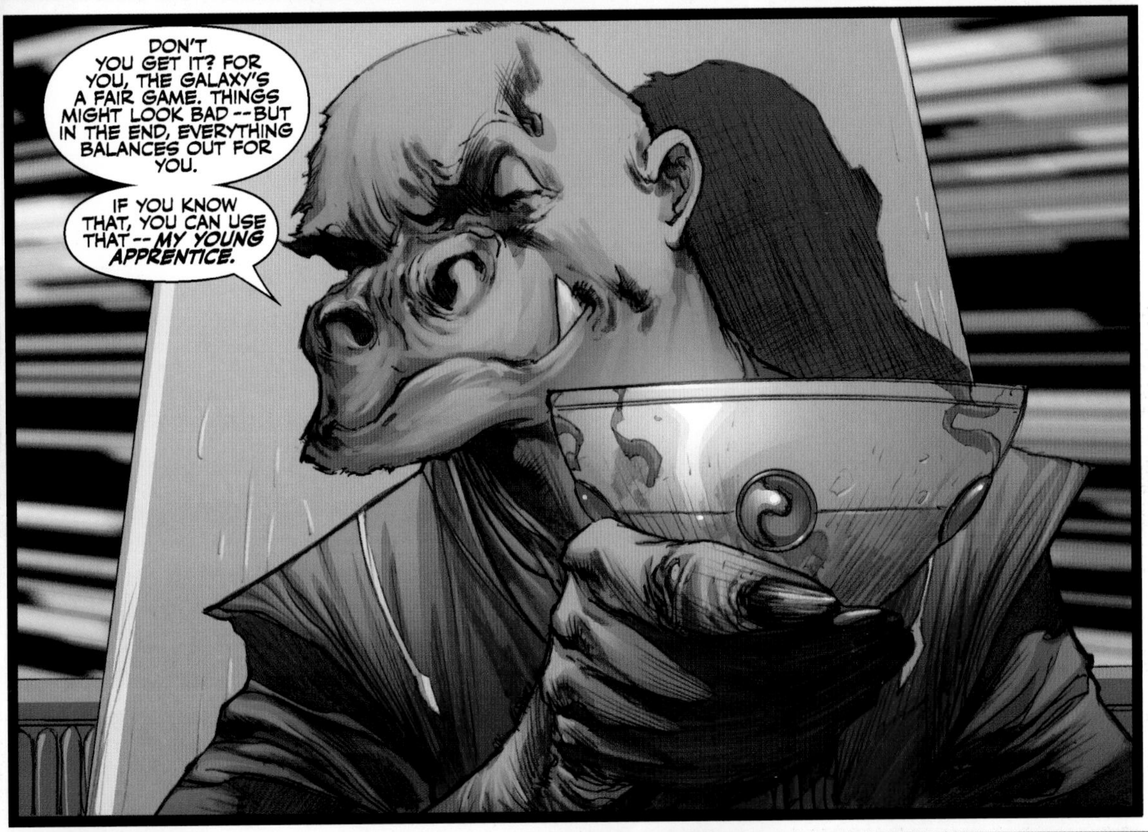
DON'T YOU GET IT? FOR YOU, THE GALAXY'S A FAIR GAME. THINGS MIGHT LOOK BAD -- BUT IN THE END, EVERYTHING BALANCES OUT FOR YOU.
IF YOU KNOW THAT, YOU CAN USE THAT -- MY YOUNG APPRENTICE.

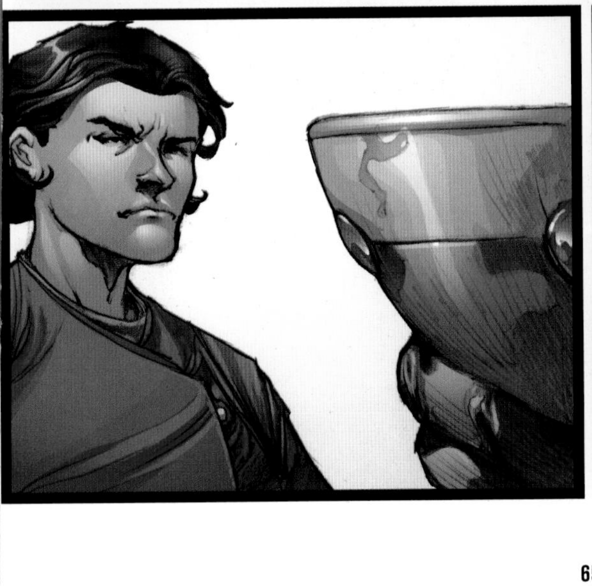

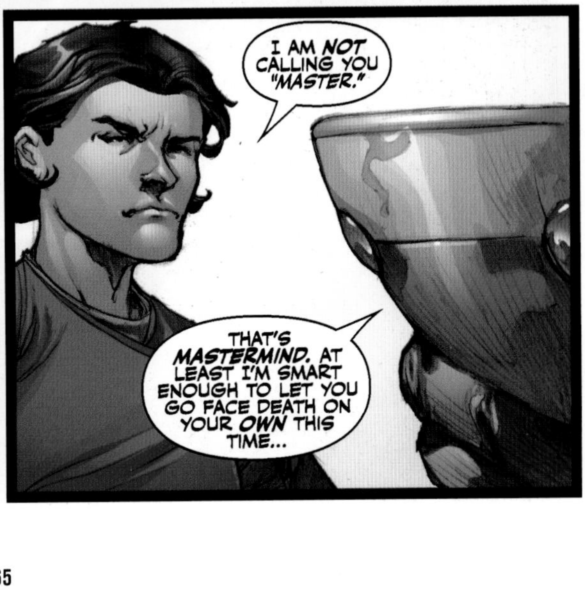
I AM NOT CALLING YOU "MASTER."
THAT'S MASTERMIND. AT LEAST I'M SMART ENOUGH TO LET YOU GO FACE DEATH ON YOUR OWN THIS TIME...

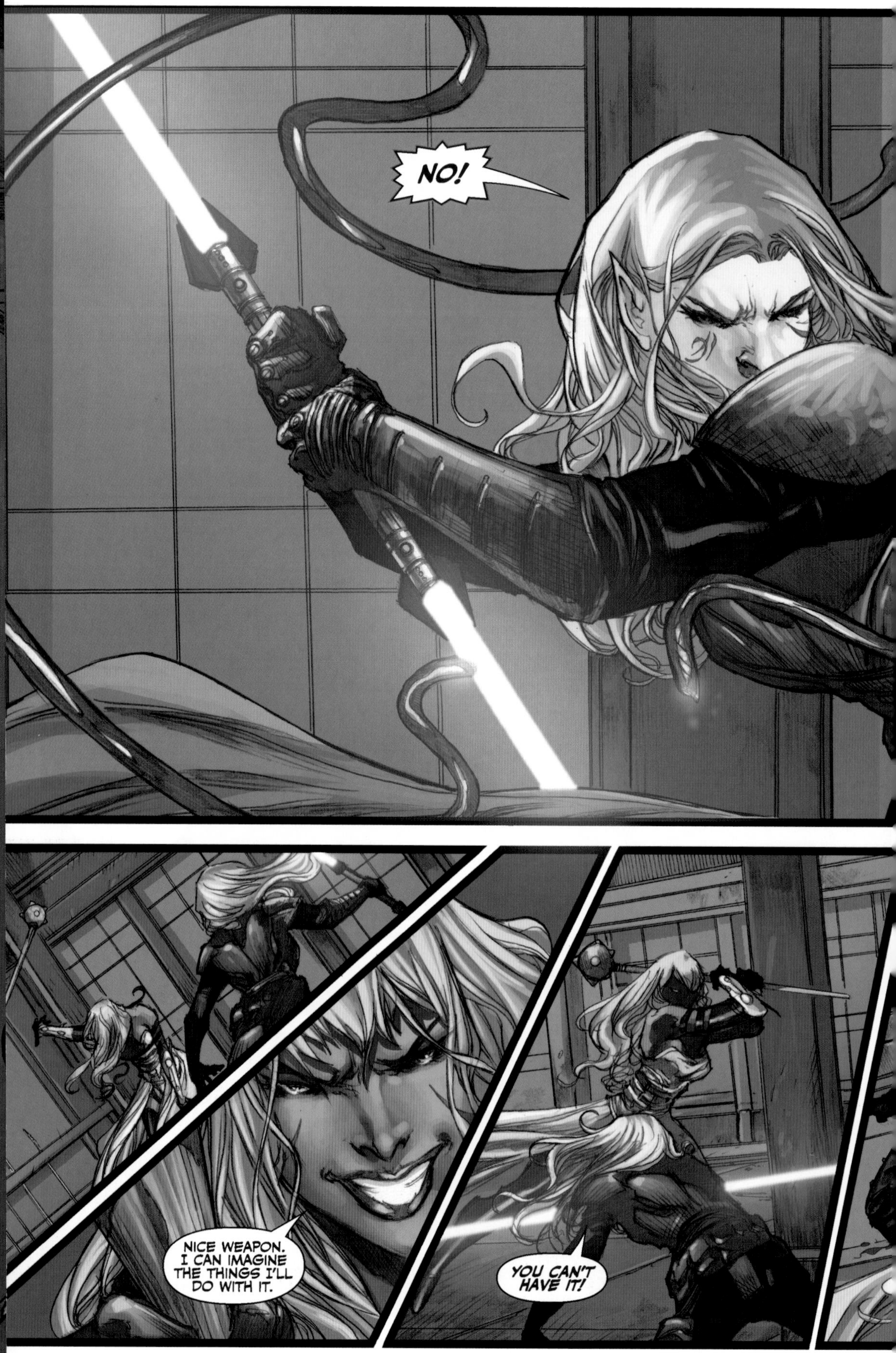
NO!
NICE WEAPON. I CAN IMAGINE THE THINGS I'LL DO WITH IT.
YOU CAN'T HAVE IT!

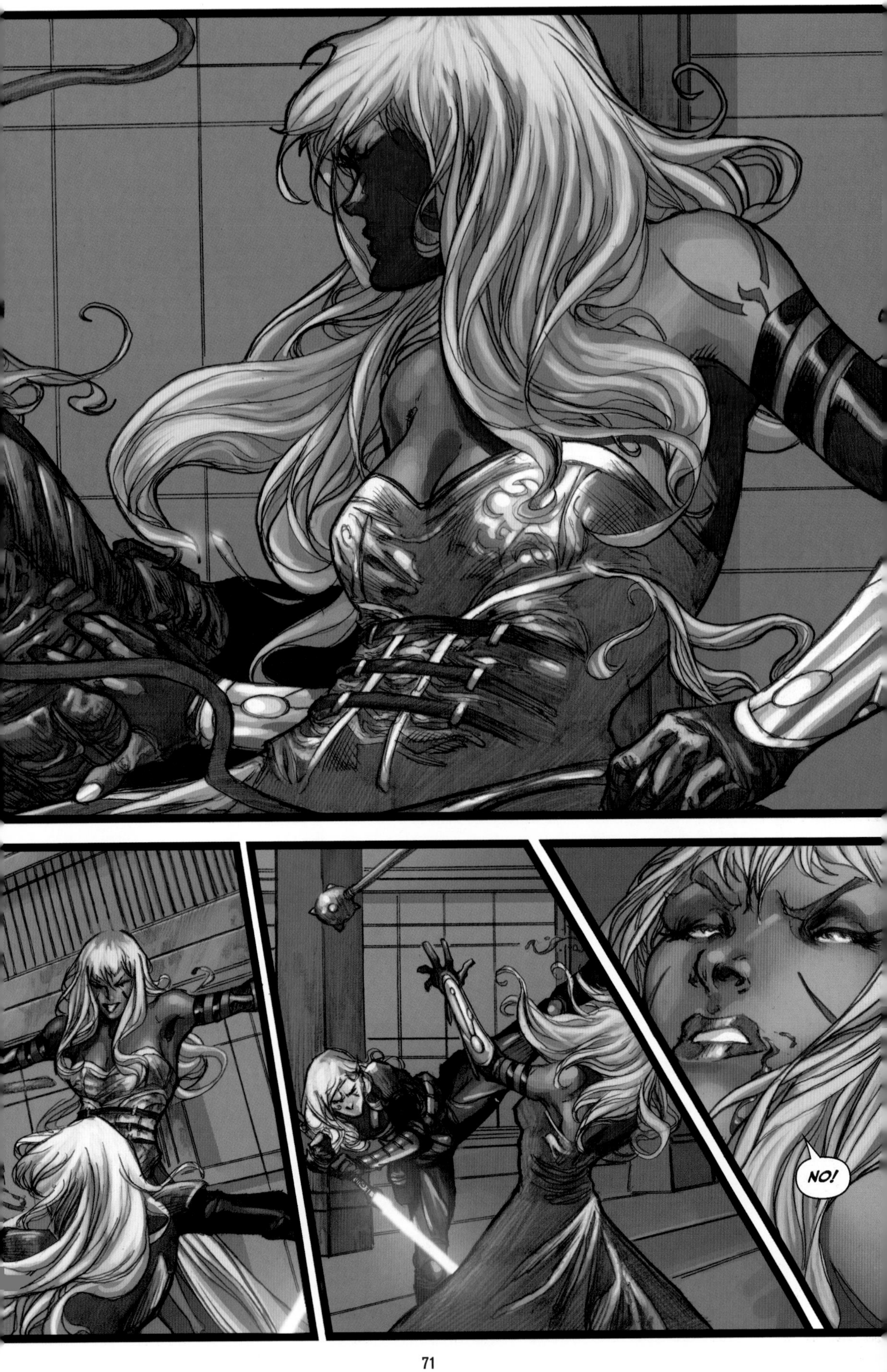
NO!

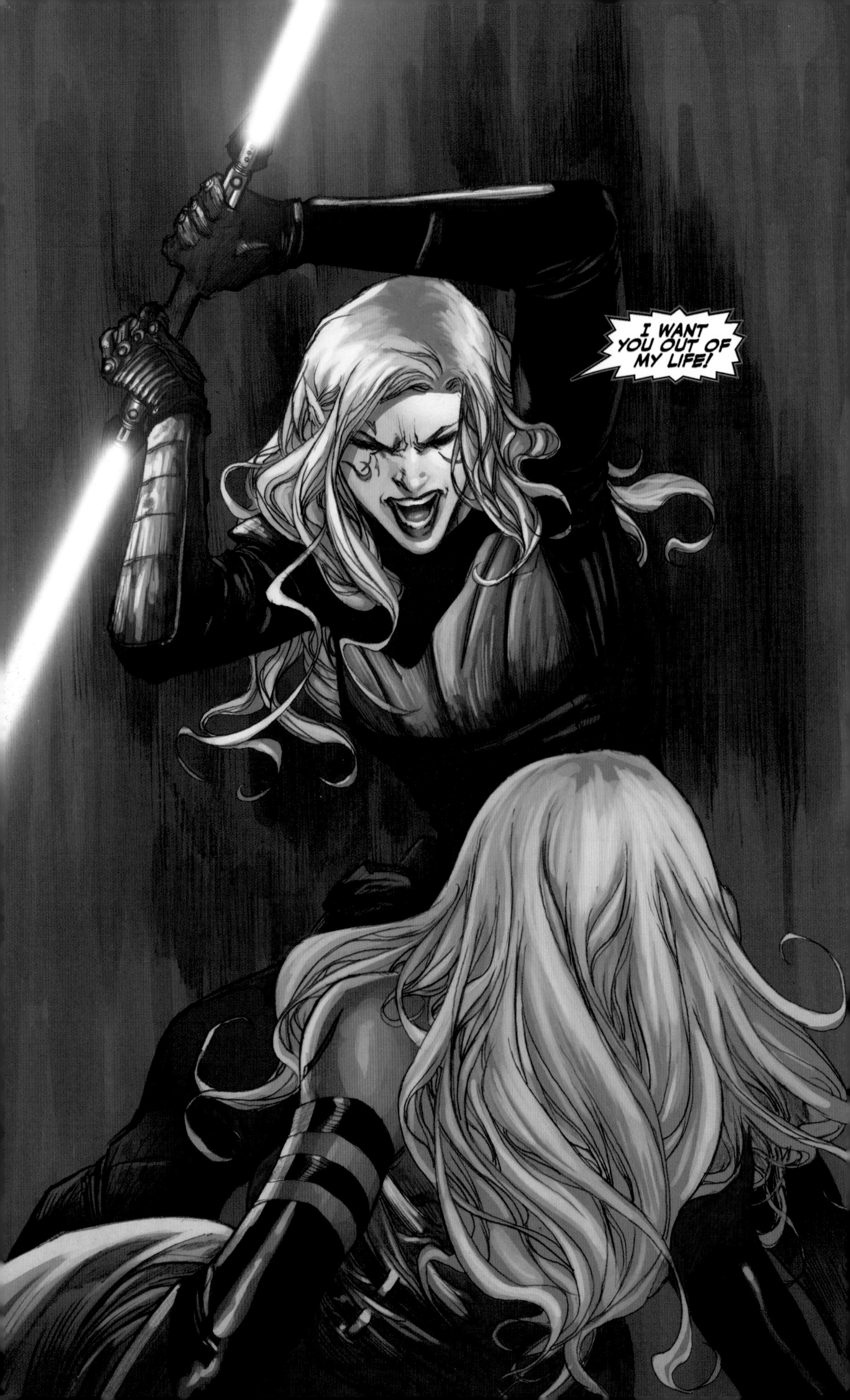
I WANT YOU OUT OF MY LIFE!

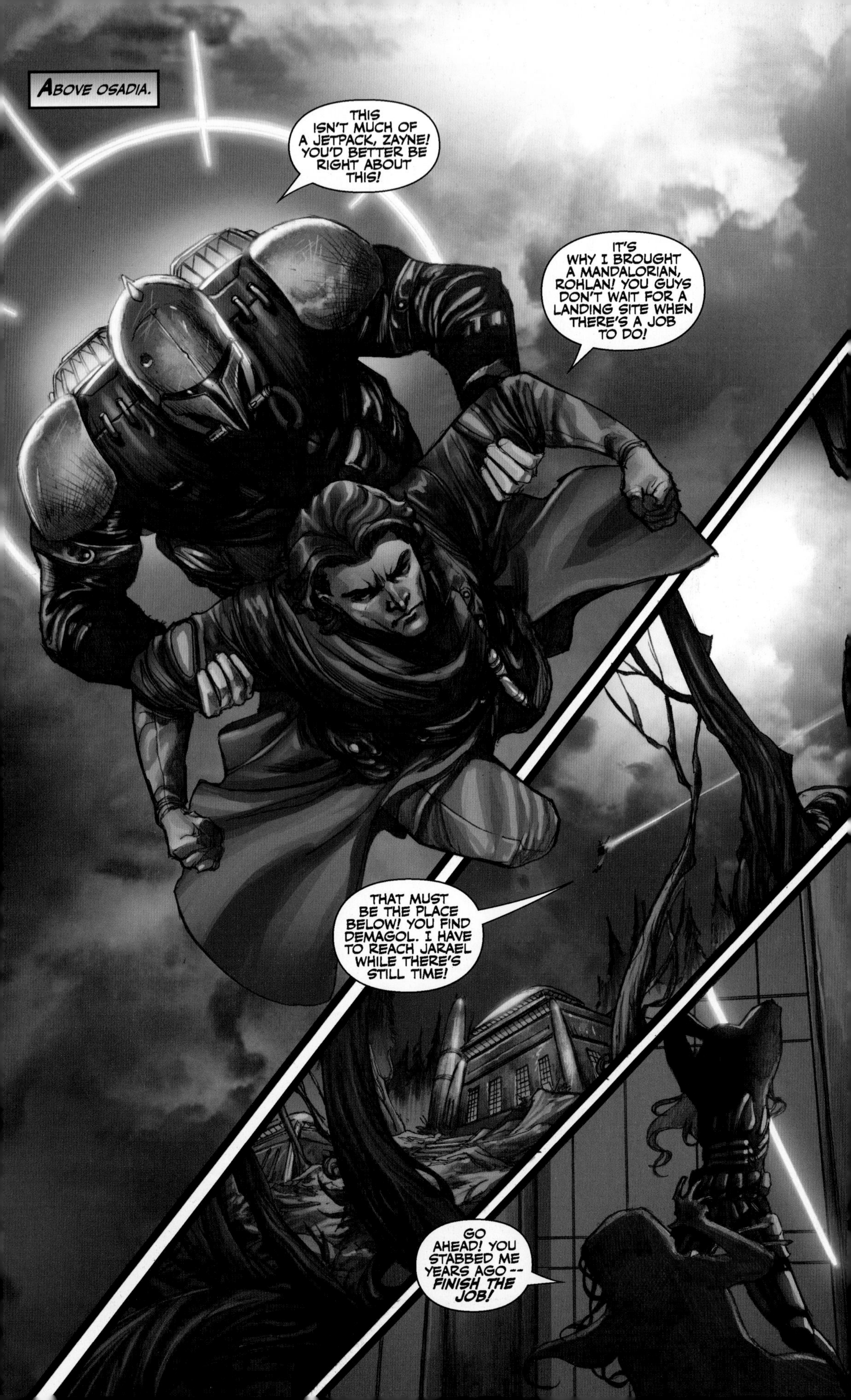
ABOVE OSADIA.
THIS ISN'T MUCH OF A JETPACK, ZAYNE! YOU'D BETTER BE RIGHT ABOUT THIS!
IT'S WHY I BROUGHT A MANDALORIAN, ROHLAN! YOU GUYS DON'T WAIT FOR A LANDING SITE WHEN THERE'S A JOB TO DO!
THAT MUST BE THE PLACE BELOW! YOU FIND DEMAGOL. I HAVE TO REACH JARAEL WHILE THERE'S STILL TIME!
GO AHEAD! YOU STABBED ME YEARS AGO -- FINISH THE JOB!

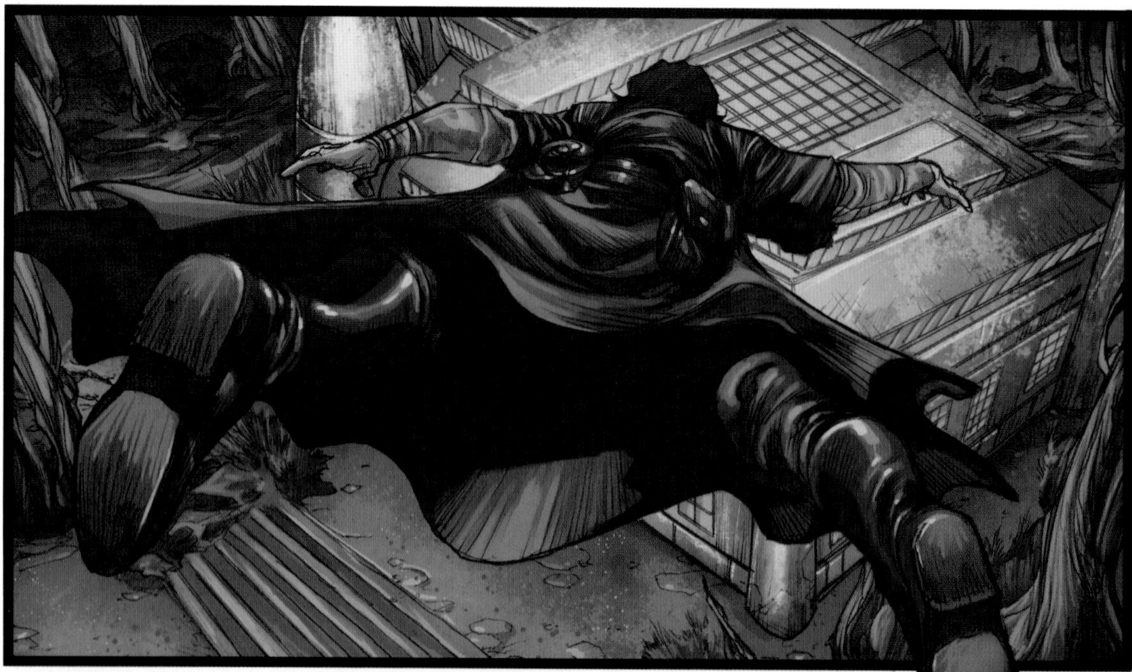

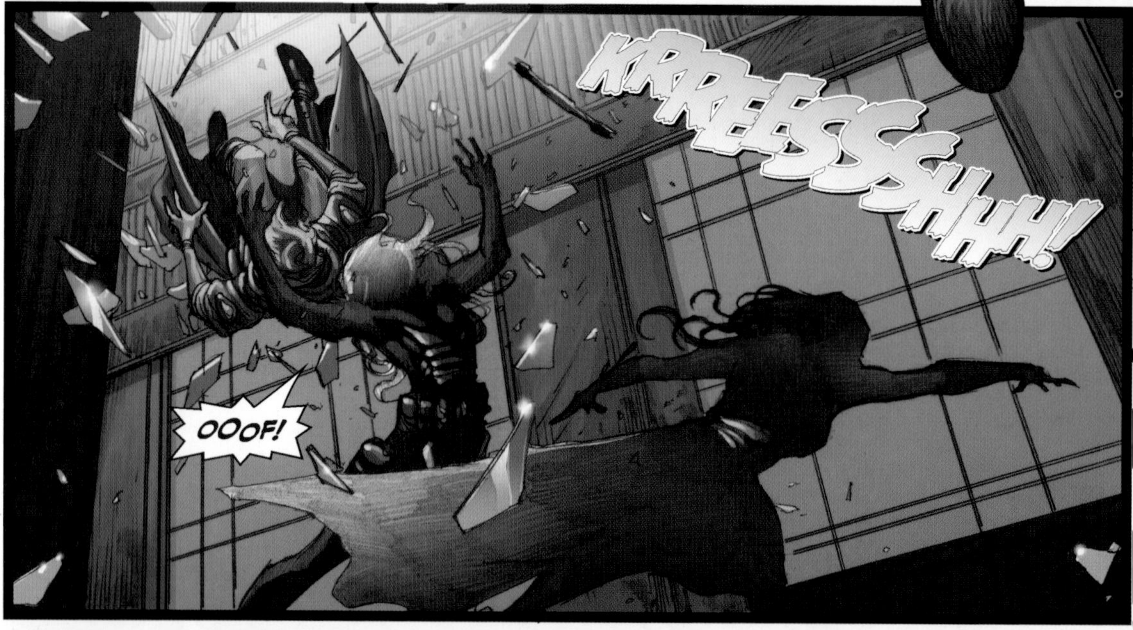
KRREESSSHHH!
OOOF!

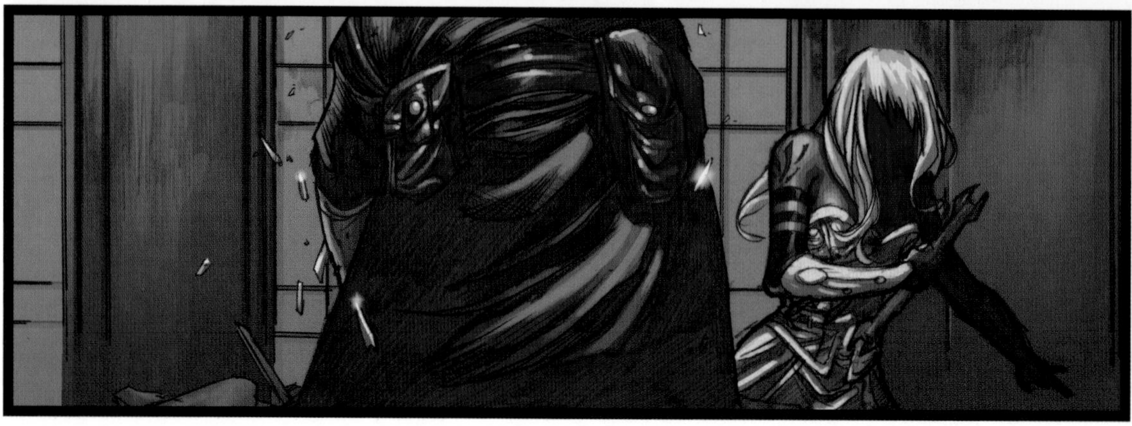

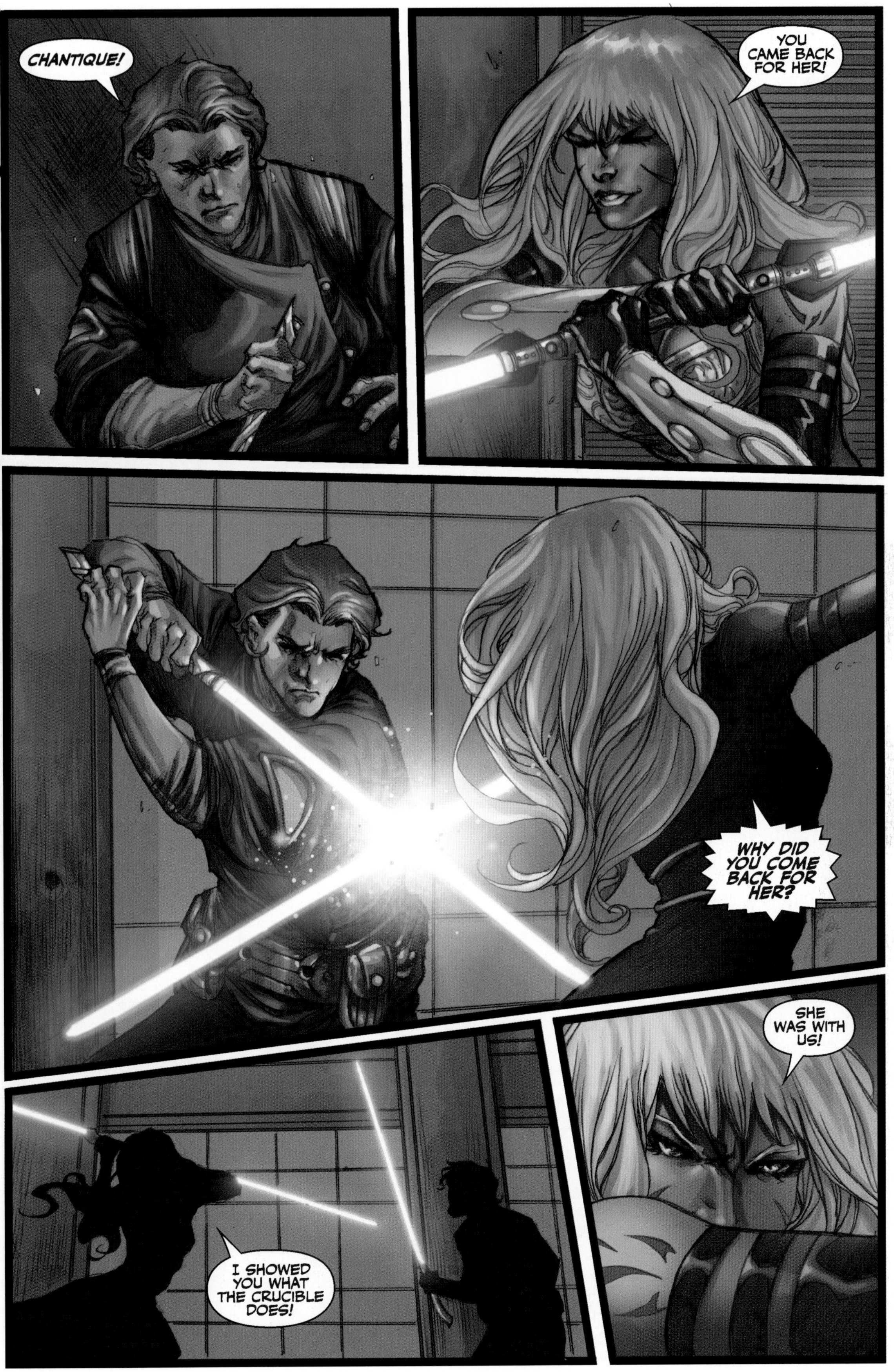
CHANTIQUE!
YOU CAME BACK FOR HER!
WHY DID YOU COME BACK FOR HER?
SHE WAS WITH US!
I SHOWED YOU WHAT THE CRUCIBLE DOES!

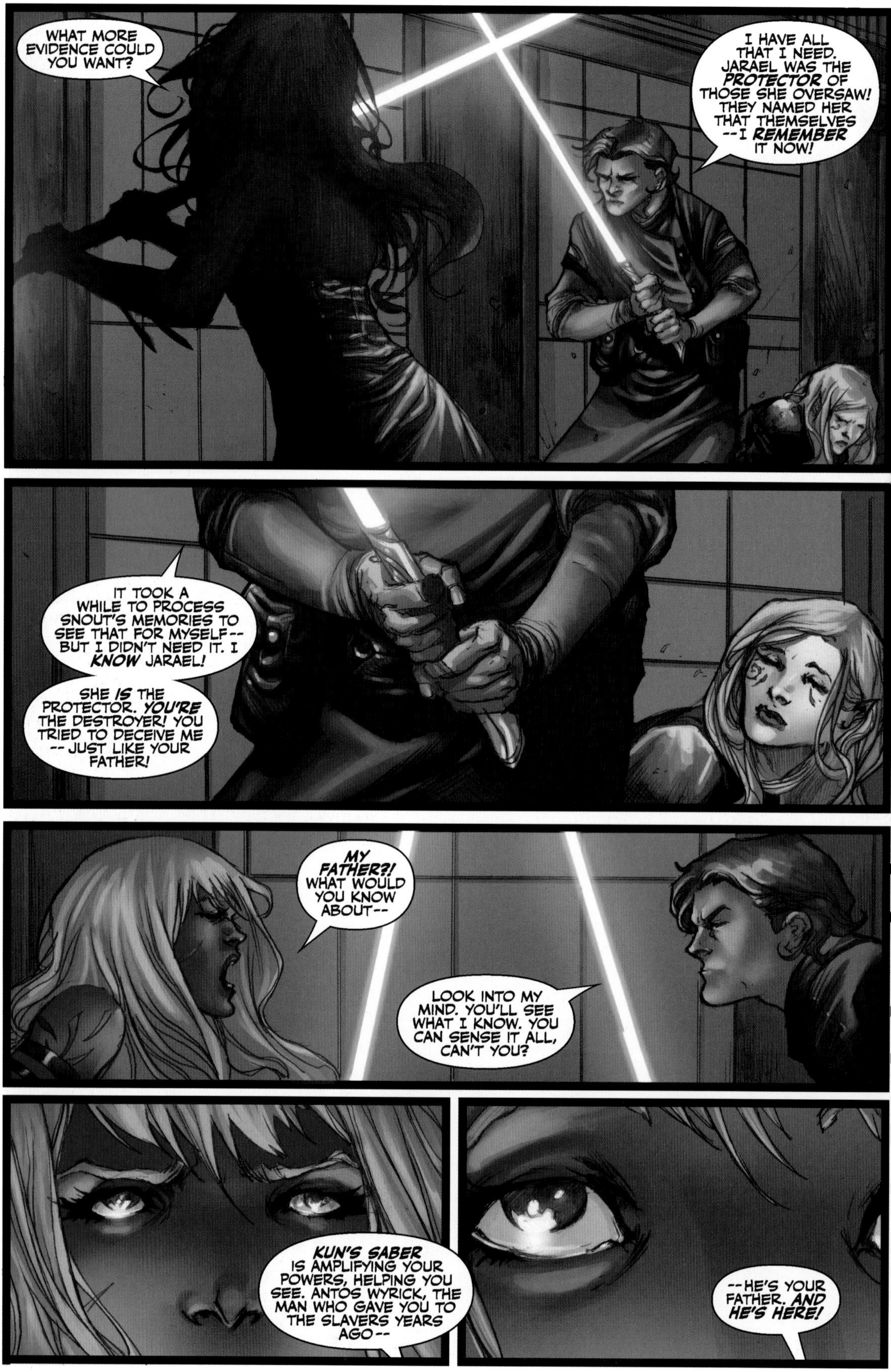
WHAT MORE EVIDENCE COULD YOU WANT?
I HAVE ALL THAT I NEED. JARAEL WAS THE *PROTECTOR* OF THOSE SHE OVERSAW! THEY NAMED HER THAT THEMSELVES --I *REMEMBER* IT NOW!
IT TOOK A WHILE TO PROCESS SNOUT'S MEMORIES TO SEE THAT FOR MYSELF-- BUT I DIDN'T NEED IT. I *KNOW* JARAEL!
SHE *IS* THE PROTECTOR. *YOU'RE* THE DESTROYER! YOU TRIED TO DECEIVE ME -- JUST LIKE YOUR FATHER!
MY FATHER?! WHAT WOULD YOU KNOW ABOUT--
LOOK INTO MY MIND. YOU'LL SEE WHAT I KNOW. YOU CAN SENSE IT ALL, CAN'T YOU?
KUN'S SABER IS AMPLIFYING YOUR POWERS, HELPING YOU SEE. ANTOS WYRICK, THE MAN WHO GAVE YOU TO THE SLAVERS YEARS AGO--
--HE'S YOUR FATHER. *AND HE'S HERE!*

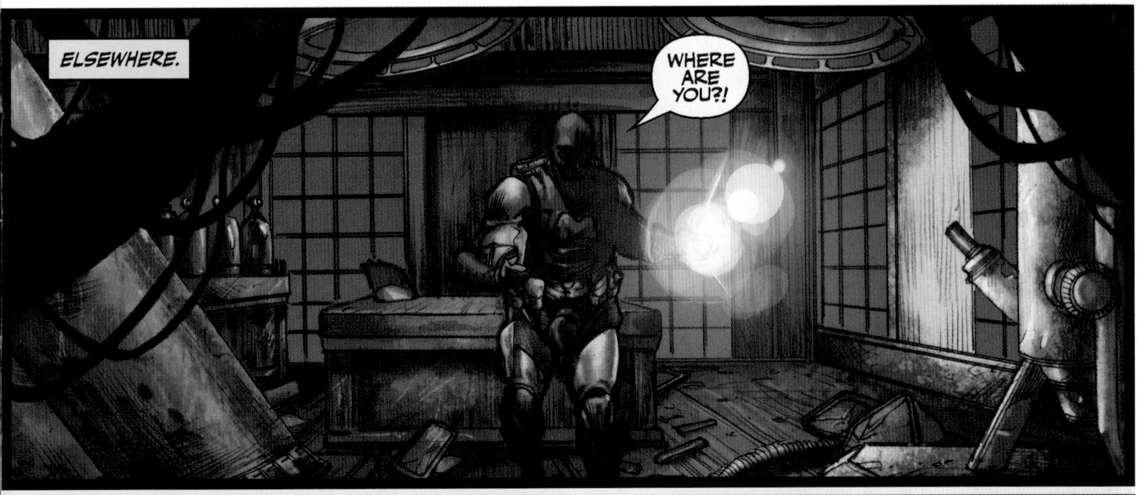
ELSEWHERE.
WHERE ARE YOU?!

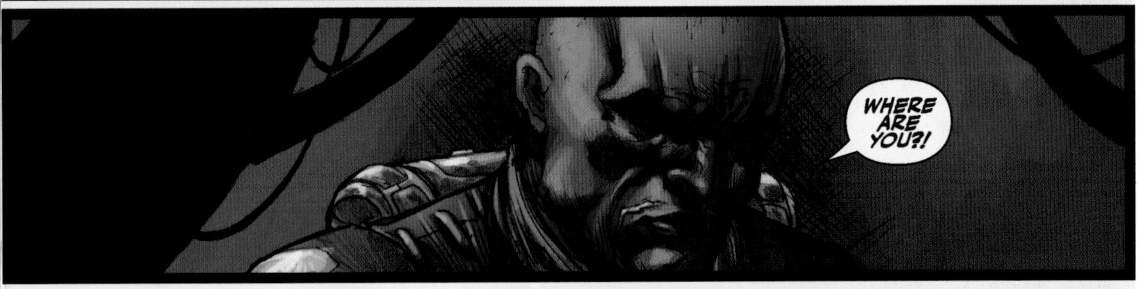
WHERE ARE YOU?!

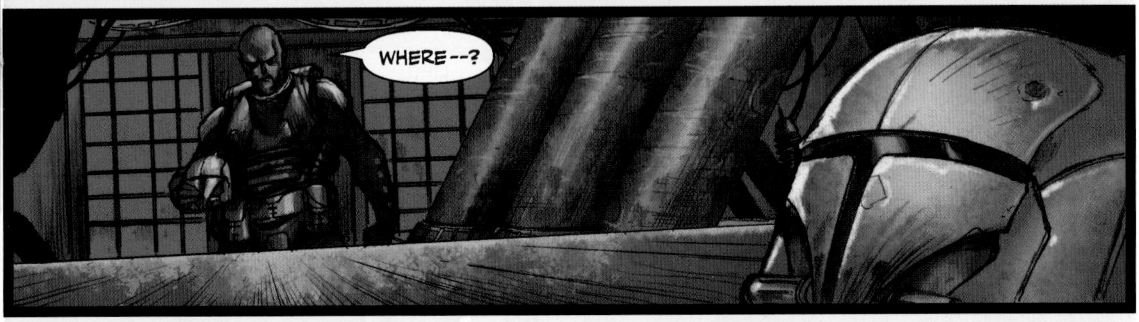
WHERE--?

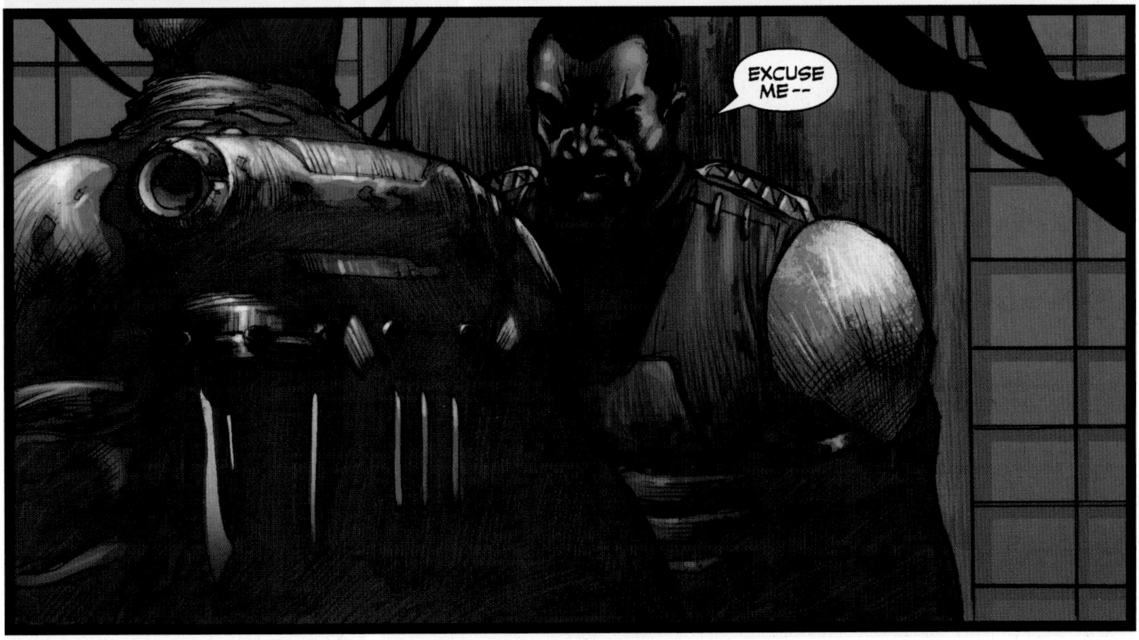
EXCUSE ME--

I DON'T GET ANY OF THIS! YOU MENTIONED WYRICK-- AND CHANTIQUE TOOK OFF LOOKING FOR HIM! AND NOW YOU SAY HE'S *DEMAGOL!*

ARE YOU INSANE? HE WAS MY MENTOR! I KNEW YOU WERE UPSET WITH ME, ZAYNE, BUT *THIS...*

I KNOW YOU DON'T THINK MUCH OF ME NOW--WITH GOOD REASON. BUT YOU HAVE TO TRUST ME.

THIS SCHOOL WAS A MANDALORIAN PROJECT--*HIS* PROJECT.

HE'S HERE TO SALVAGE IT! THERE WAS SOMETHING *DIFFERENT* ABOUT HIS STUDENTS--

--YOU'RE ALL TOUCHED WITH THE FORCE IN A POWERFUL WAY. IT'S WHY I'M GLAD YOU LOST THAT LIGHTSABER. IT'S AN *EVIL ARTIFACT!*

IN THE HANDS OF A FORCE USER, IT COULD REALLY CHANGE THEM! YOU COULD HAVE KILLED CHANTIQUE -- AND THEN WORSE!

BUT...I DIDN'T. I WANTED TO, BUT I DIDN'T. I JUST WANTED HER TO LEAVE ME ALONE.

I DIDN'T FEEL ANYTHING FROM THE LIGHTSABER -- EXCEPT MAYBE THAT IT'S REALLY TOUGH TO USE.

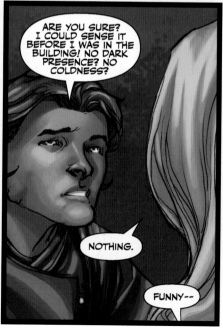

ARE YOU SURE? I COULD SENSE IT BEFORE I WAS IN THE BUILDING! NO DARK PRESENCE? NO COLDNESS?

NOTHING.

FUNNY--

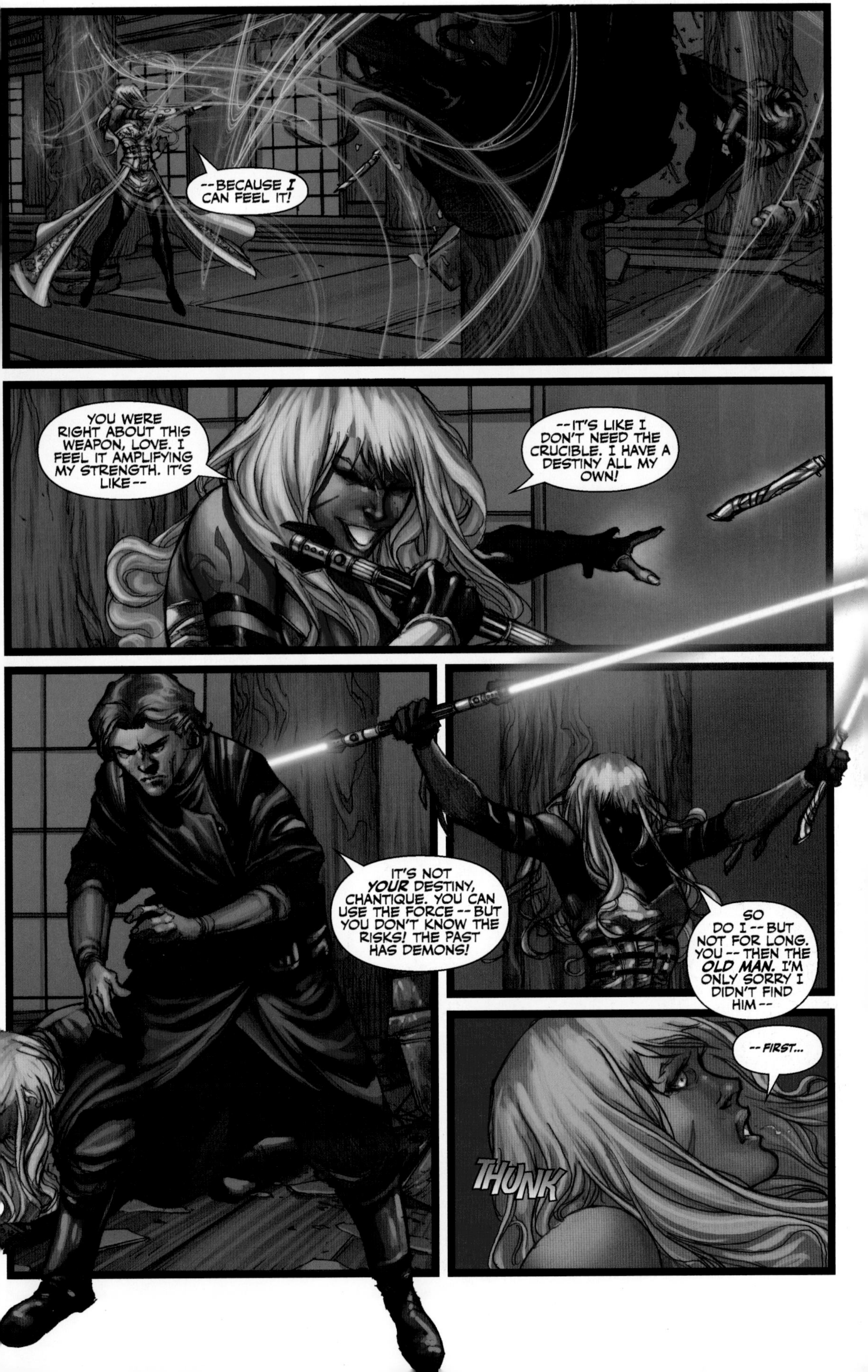
--BECAUSE I CAN FEEL IT!
YOU WERE RIGHT ABOUT THIS WEAPON, LOVE. I FEEL IT AMPLIFYING MY STRENGTH. IT'S LIKE--
--IT'S LIKE I DON'T NEED THE CRUCIBLE. I HAVE A DESTINY ALL MY OWN!
IT'S NOT YOUR DESTINY, CHANTIQUE. YOU CAN USE THE FORCE -- BUT YOU DON'T KNOW THE RISKS! THE PAST HAS DEMONS!
SO DO I -- BUT NOT FOR LONG. YOU -- THEN THE OLD MAN. I'M ONLY SORRY I DIDN'T FIND HIM--
--FIRST...
THUNK

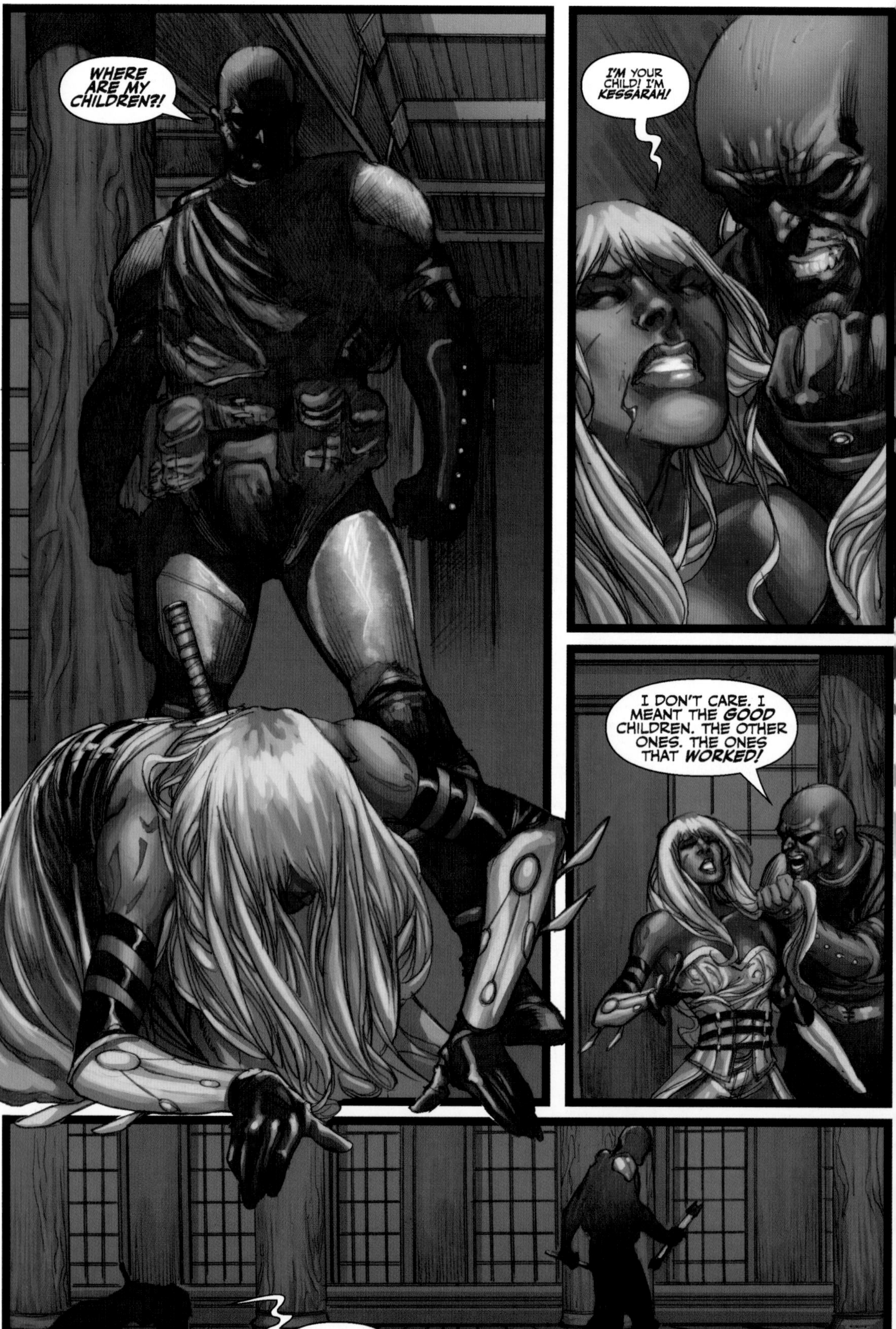
WHERE ARE MY CHILDREN?!
I'M YOUR CHILD! I'M KESSARAH!
I DON'T CARE. I MEANT THE GOOD CHILDREN. THE OTHER ONES. THE ONES THAT WORKED!
THEY'RE... IN THE SCHOOLYARD.

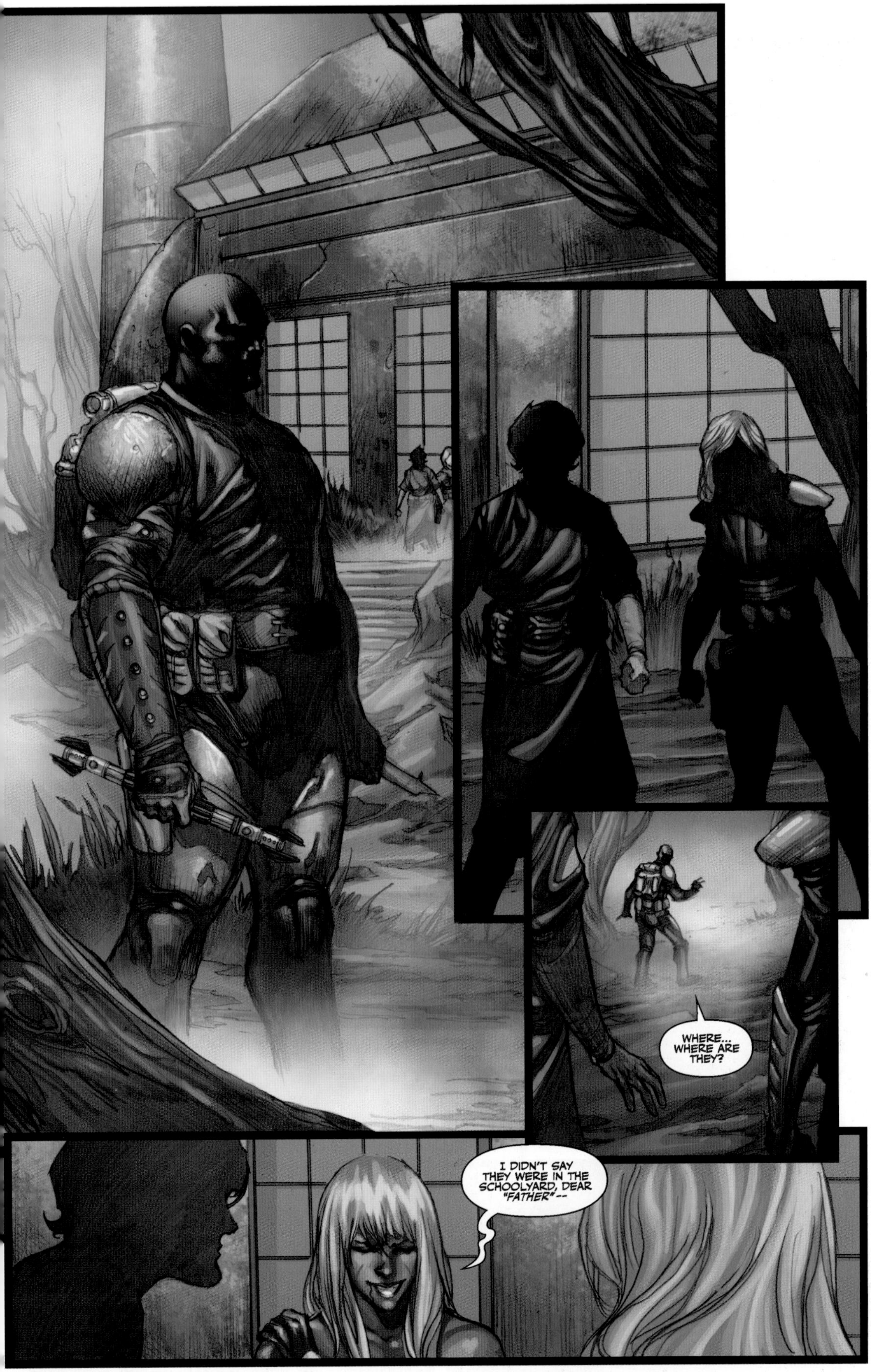
WHERE... WHERE ARE THEY?
I DIDN'T SAY THEY WERE IN THE SCHOOLYARD, DEAR "FATHER"--

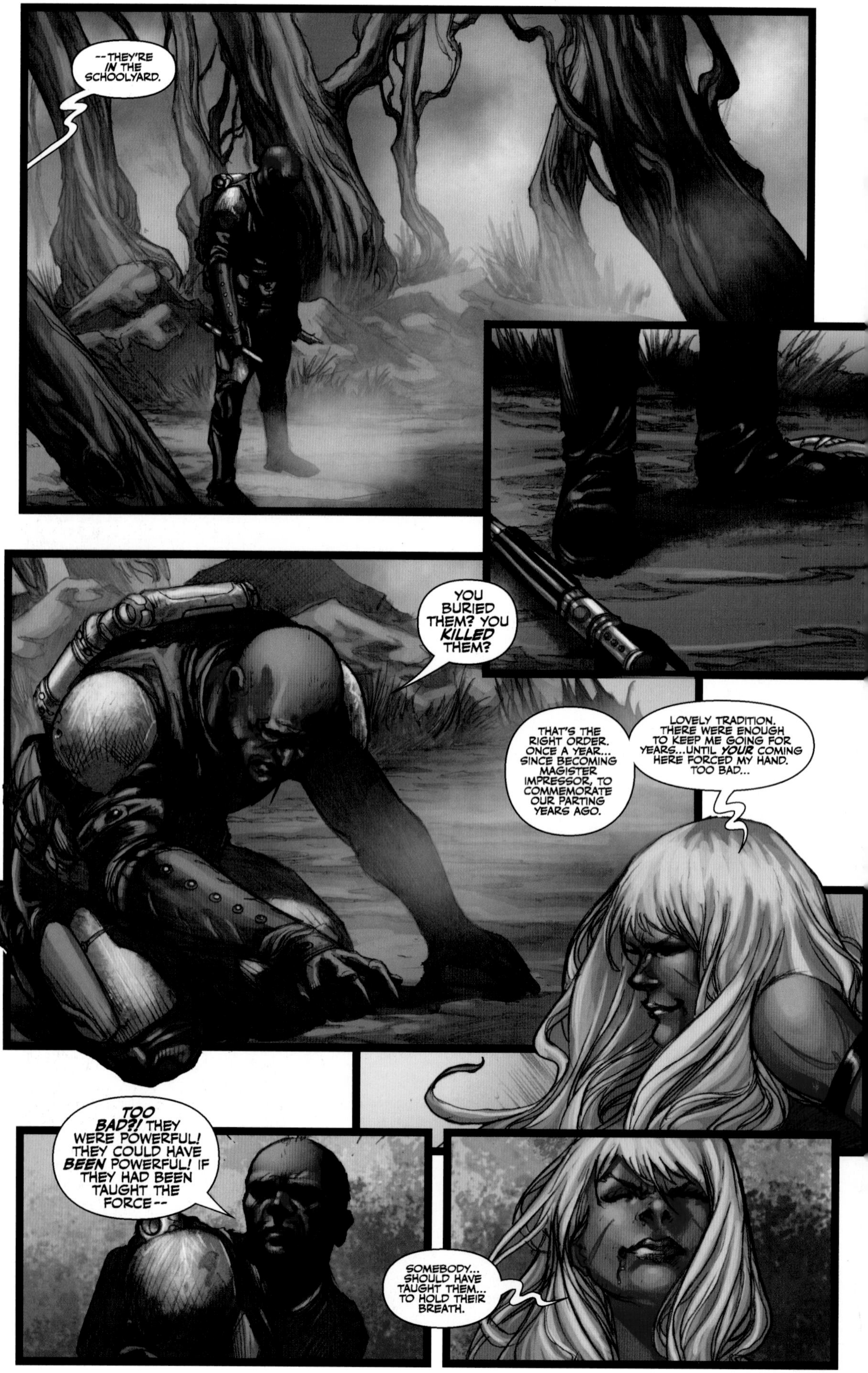
--THEY'RE IN THE SCHOOLYARD.
YOU BURIED THEM? YOU KILLED THEM?
THAT'S THE RIGHT ORDER. ONCE A YEAR... SINCE BECOMING MAGISTER IMPRESSOR, TO COMMEMORATE OUR PARTING YEARS AGO.
LOVELY TRADITION. THERE WERE ENOUGH TO KEEP ME GOING FOR YEARS...UNTIL YOUR COMING HERE FORCED MY HAND. TOO BAD...
TOO BAD?! THEY WERE POWERFUL! THEY COULD HAVE BEEN POWERFUL! IF THEY HAD BEEN TAUGHT THE FORCE--
SOMEBODY... SHOULD HAVE TAUGHT THEM... TO HOLD THEIR BREATH.

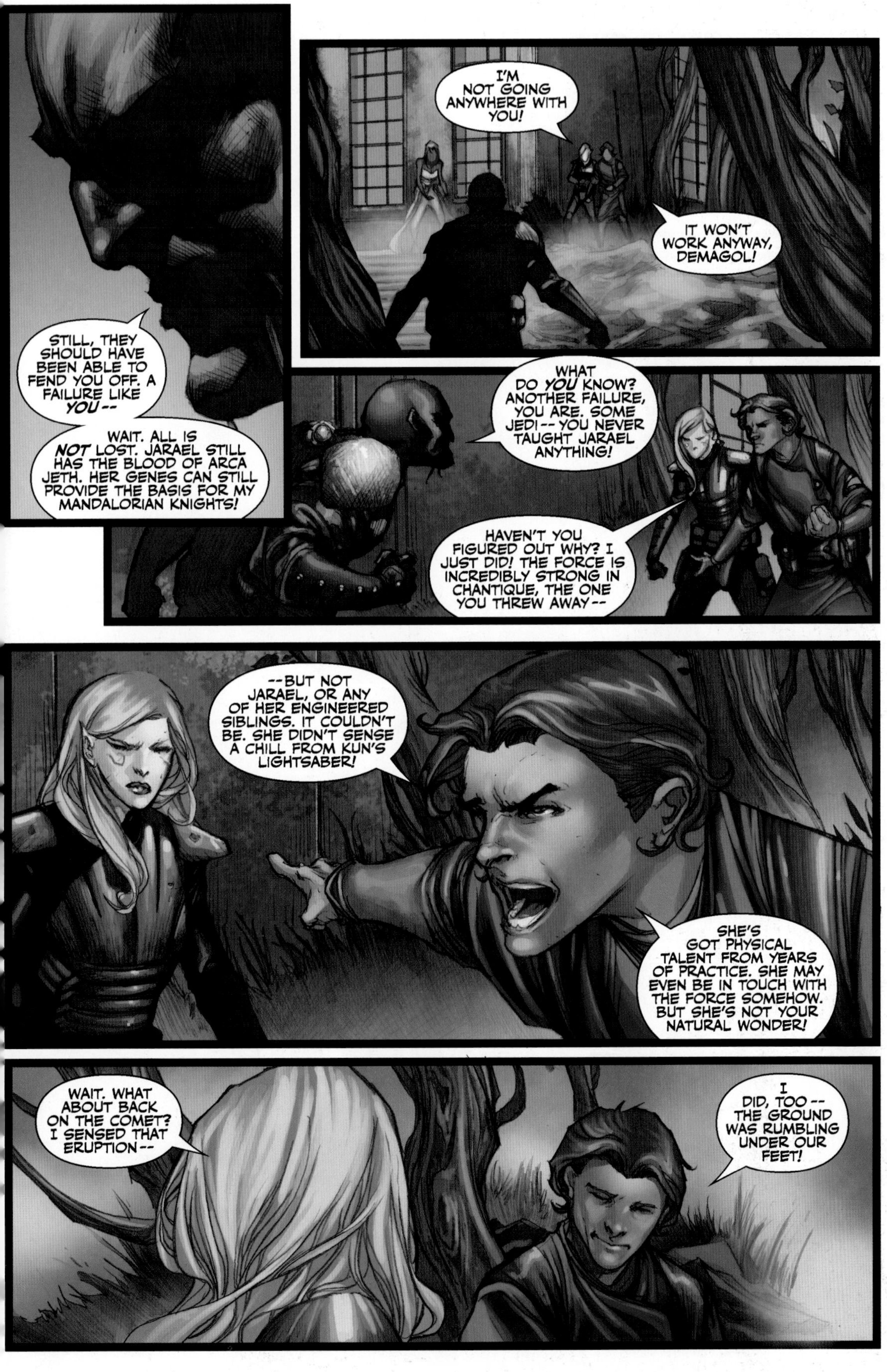
STILL, THEY SHOULD HAVE BEEN ABLE TO FEND YOU OFF. A FAILURE LIKE *YOU*--
WAIT. ALL IS *NOT* LOST. JARAEL STILL HAS THE BLOOD OF ARCA JETH. HER GENES CAN STILL PROVIDE THE BASIS FOR MY MANDALORIAN KNIGHTS!
I'M NOT GOING ANYWHERE WITH YOU!
IT WON'T WORK ANYWAY, DEMAGOL!
WHAT DO *YOU* KNOW? ANOTHER FAILURE, YOU ARE. SOME JEDI--YOU NEVER TAUGHT JARAEL ANYTHING!
HAVEN'T YOU FIGURED OUT WHY? I JUST DID! THE FORCE IS INCREDIBLY STRONG IN CHANTIQUE, THE ONE YOU THREW AWAY--
--BUT NOT JARAEL, OR ANY OF HER ENGINEERED SIBLINGS. IT COULDN'T BE. SHE DIDN'T SENSE A CHILL FROM KUN'S LIGHTSABER!
SHE'S GOT PHYSICAL TALENT FROM YEARS OF PRACTICE. SHE MAY EVEN BE IN TOUCH WITH THE FORCE SOMEHOW. BUT SHE'S NOT YOUR NATURAL WONDER!
WAIT. WHAT ABOUT BACK ON THE COMET? I SENSED THAT ERUPTION--
I DID, TOO--THE GROUND WAS RUMBLING UNDER OUR FEET!

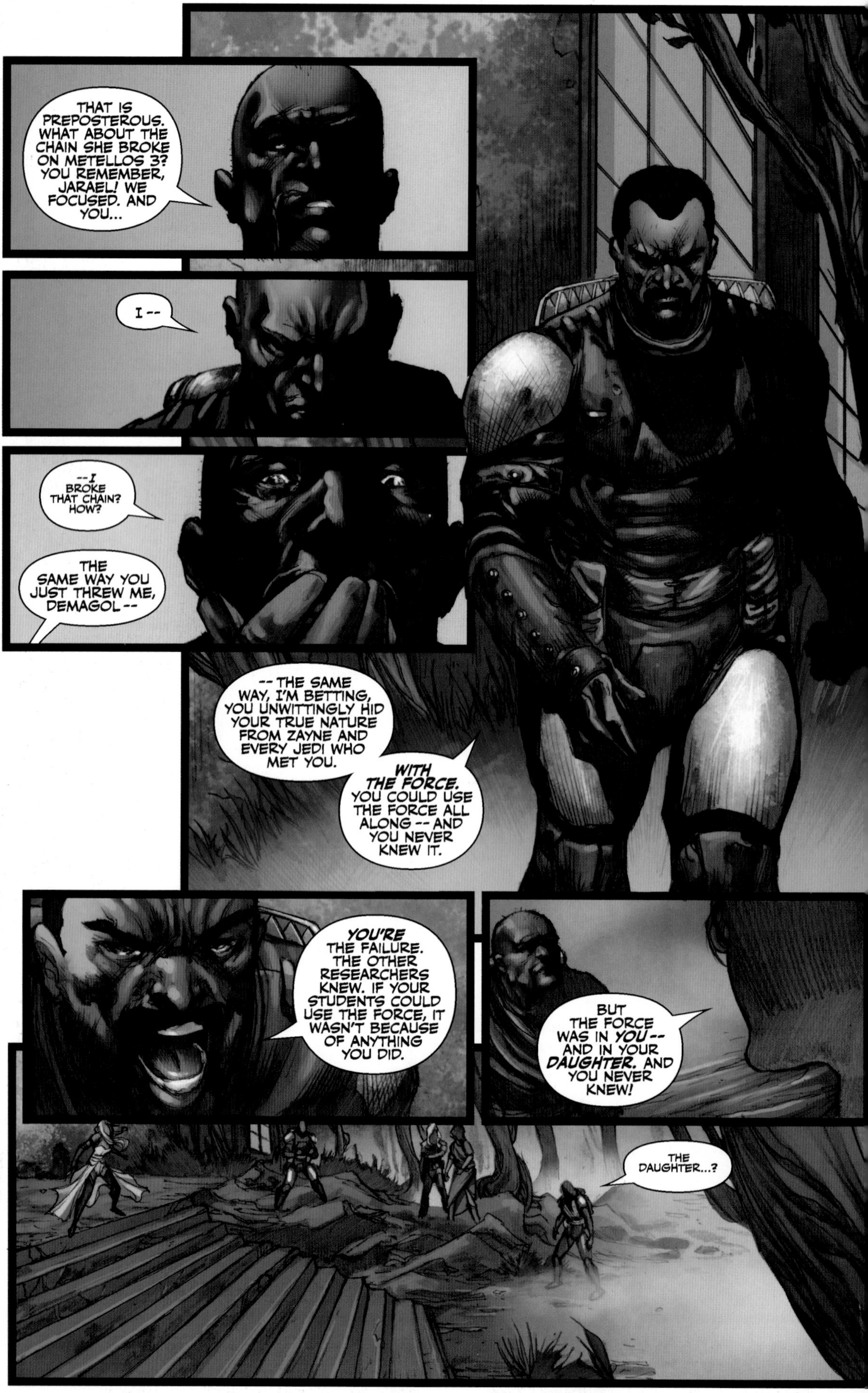
THAT IS PREPOSTEROUS. WHAT ABOUT THE CHAIN SHE BROKE ON METELLOS 3? YOU REMEMBER, JARAEL! WE FOCUSED. AND YOU...
I --
--I BROKE THAT CHAIN? HOW?
THE SAME WAY YOU JUST THREW ME, DEMAGOL --
-- THE SAME WAY, I'M BETTING, YOU UNWITTINGLY HID YOUR TRUE NATURE FROM ZAYNE AND EVERY JEDI WHO MET YOU.
WITH THE FORCE. YOU COULD USE THE FORCE ALL ALONG -- AND YOU NEVER KNEW IT.
YOU'RE THE FAILURE. THE OTHER RESEARCHERS KNEW. IF YOUR STUDENTS COULD USE THE FORCE, IT WASN'T BECAUSE OF ANYTHING YOU DID.
BUT THE FORCE WAS IN YOU -- AND IN YOUR DAUGHTER. AND YOU NEVER KNEW!
THE DAUGHTER...?

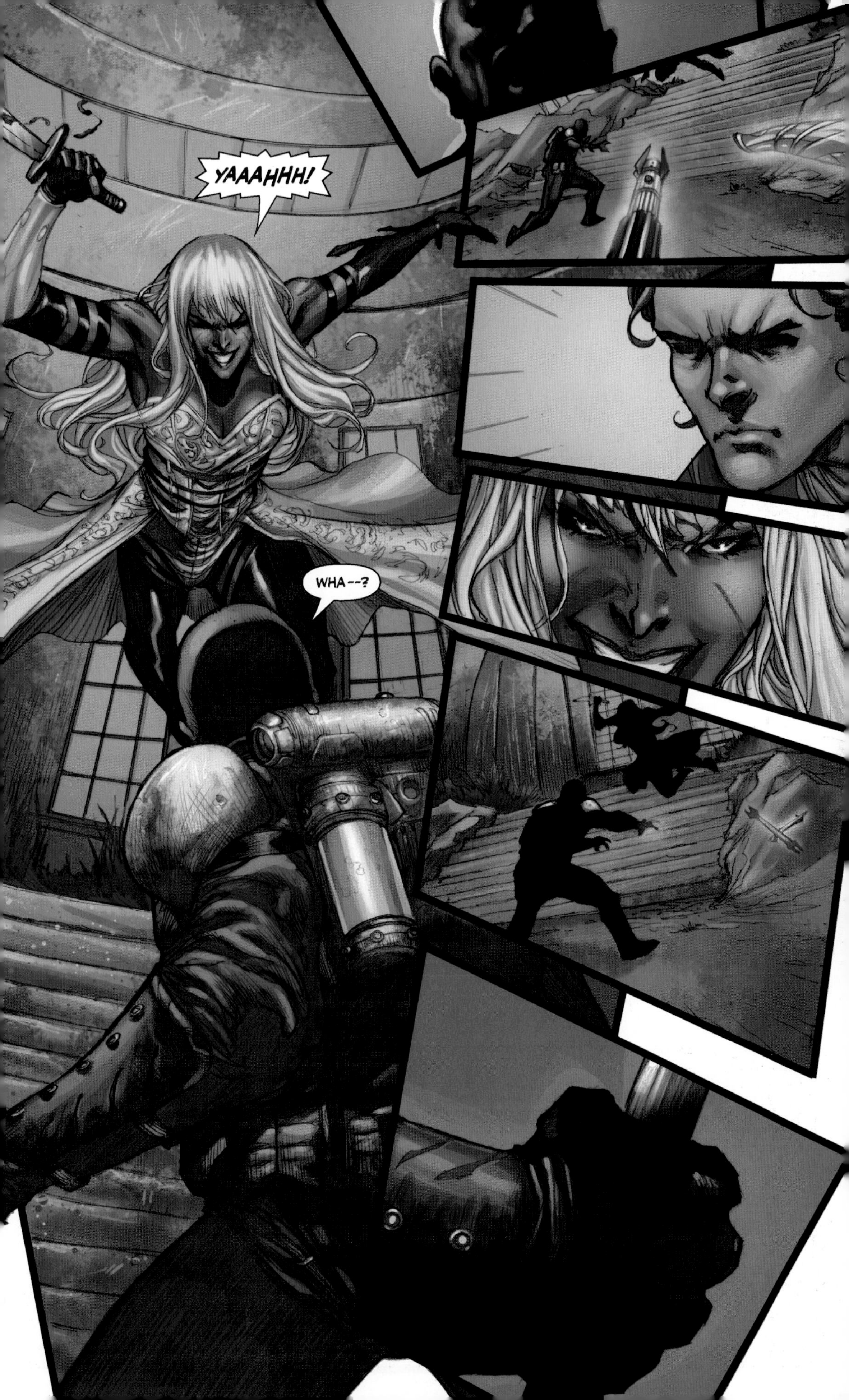
YAAAHHH!
WHA--?

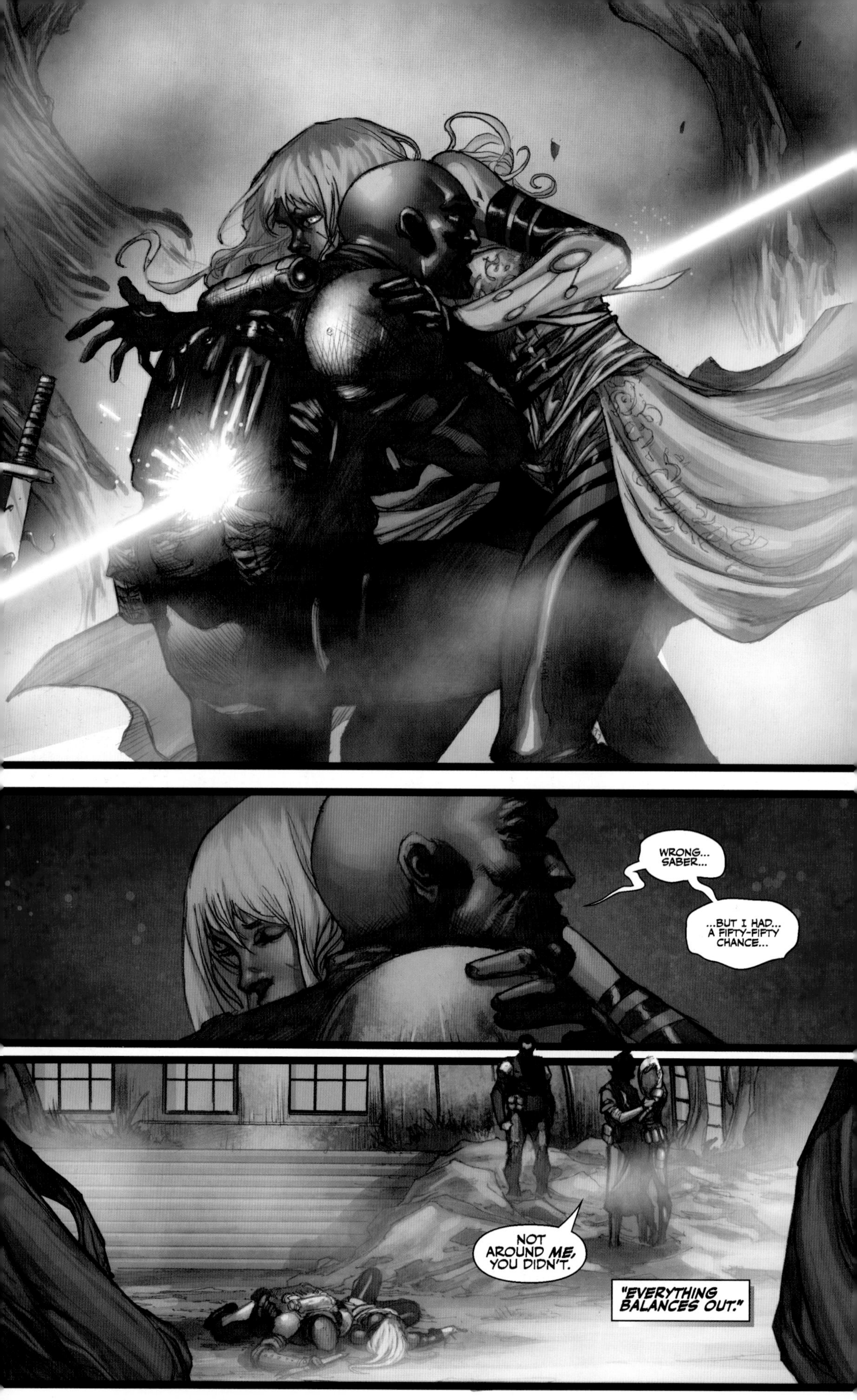
WRONG... SABER...
...BUT I HAD... A FIFTY-FIFTY CHANCE...
NOT AROUND *ME,* YOU DIDN'T.
"EVERYTHING BALANCES OUT."

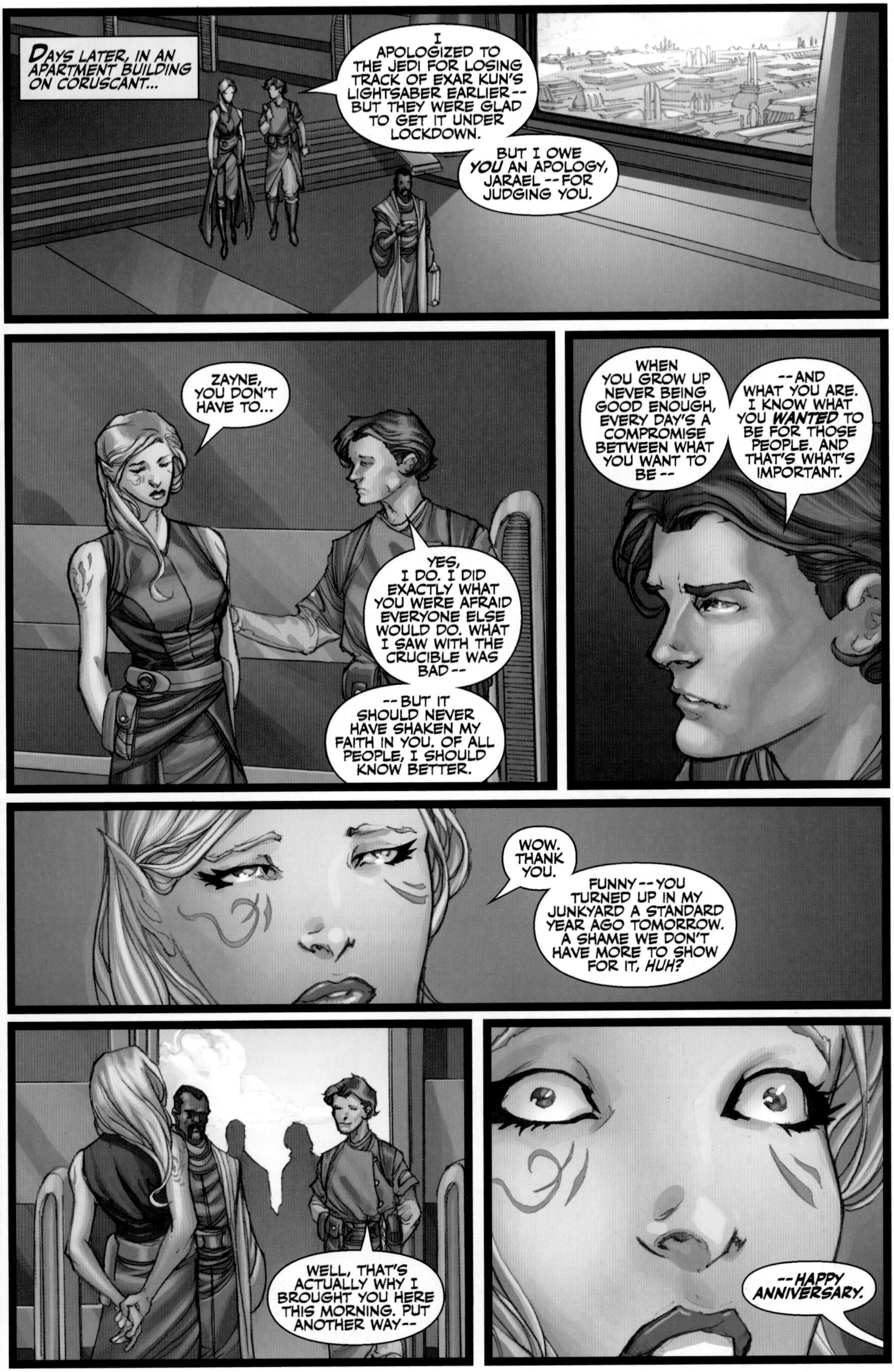
DAYS LATER, IN AN APARTMENT BUILDING ON CORUSCANT...
I APOLOGIZED TO THE JEDI FOR LOSING TRACK OF EXAR KUN'S LIGHTSABER EARLIER-- BUT THEY WERE GLAD TO GET IT UNDER LOCKDOWN.
BUT I OWE *YOU* AN APOLOGY, JARAEL --FOR JUDGING YOU.
ZAYNE, YOU DON'T HAVE TO...
YES, I DO. I DID EXACTLY WHAT YOU WERE AFRAID EVERYONE ELSE WOULD DO. WHAT I SAW WITH THE CRUCIBLE WAS BAD--
--BUT IT SHOULD NEVER HAVE SHAKEN MY FAITH IN YOU. OF ALL PEOPLE, I SHOULD KNOW BETTER.
WHEN YOU GROW UP NEVER BEING GOOD ENOUGH, EVERY DAY'S A COMPROMISE BETWEEN WHAT YOU WANT TO BE--
--AND WHAT YOU ARE. I KNOW WHAT YOU *WANTED* TO BE FOR THOSE PEOPLE. AND THAT'S WHAT'S IMPORTANT.
WOW. THANK YOU.
FUNNY--YOU TURNED UP IN MY JUNKYARD A STANDARD YEAR AGO TOMORROW. A SHAME WE DON'T HAVE MORE TO SHOW FOR IT, *HUH?*
WELL, THAT'S ACTUALLY WHY I BROUGHT YOU HERE THIS MORNING. PUT ANOTHER WAY--
--HAPPY ANNIVERSARY.

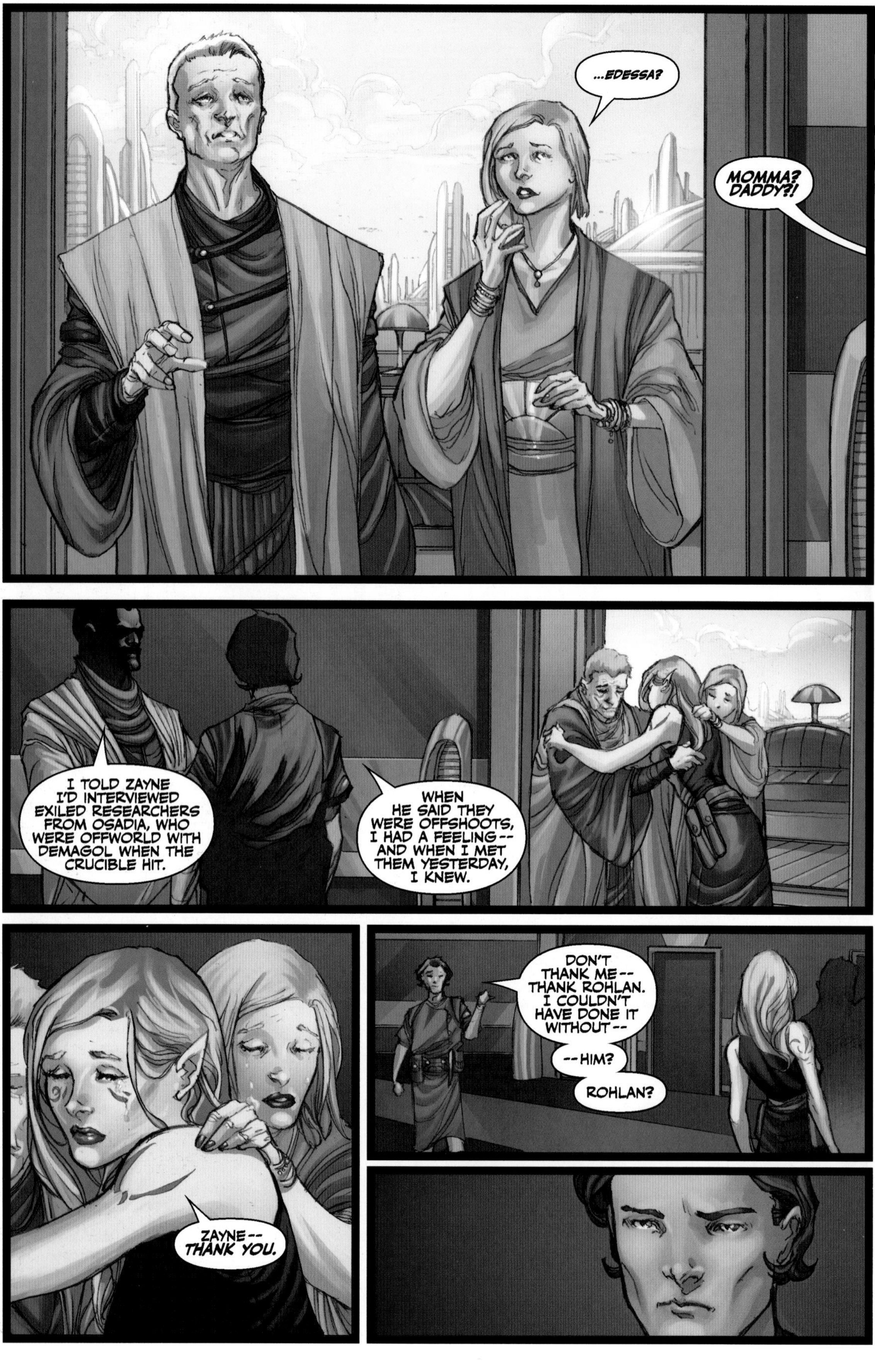
...EDESSA?
MOMMA? DADDY?!
I TOLD ZAYNE I'D INTERVIEWED EXILED RESEARCHERS FROM OSADIA, WHO WERE OFFWORLD WITH DEMAGOL WHEN THE CRUCIBLE HIT.
WHEN HE SAID THEY WERE OFFSHOOTS, I HAD A FEELING-- AND WHEN I MET THEM YESTERDAY, I KNEW.
ZAYNE-- THANK YOU.
DON'T THANK ME-- THANK ROHLAN. I COULDN'T HAVE DONE IT WITHOUT--
--HIM?
ROHLAN?

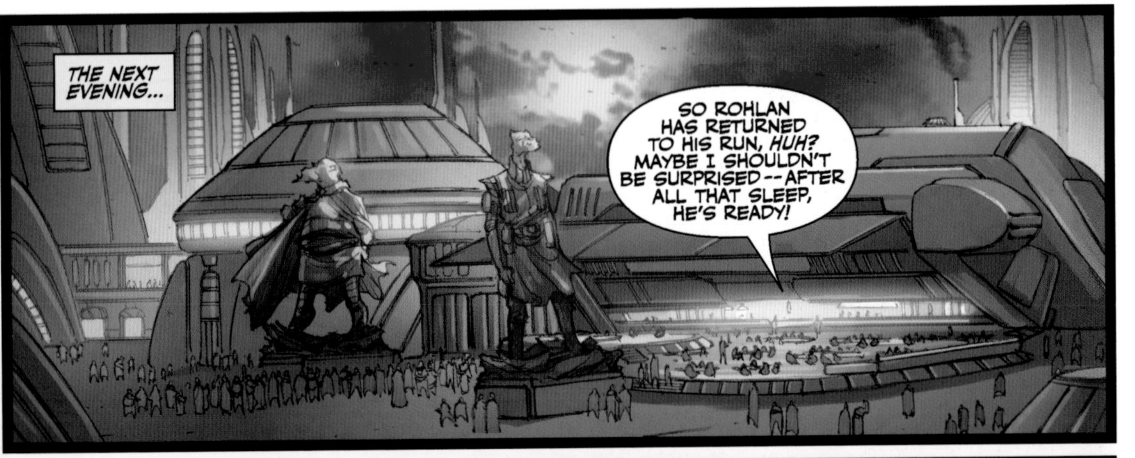
THE NEXT EVENING...
SO ROHLAN HAS RETURNED TO HIS RUN, *HUH?* MAYBE I SHOULDN'T BE SURPRISED -- AFTER ALL THAT SLEEP, HE'S READY!

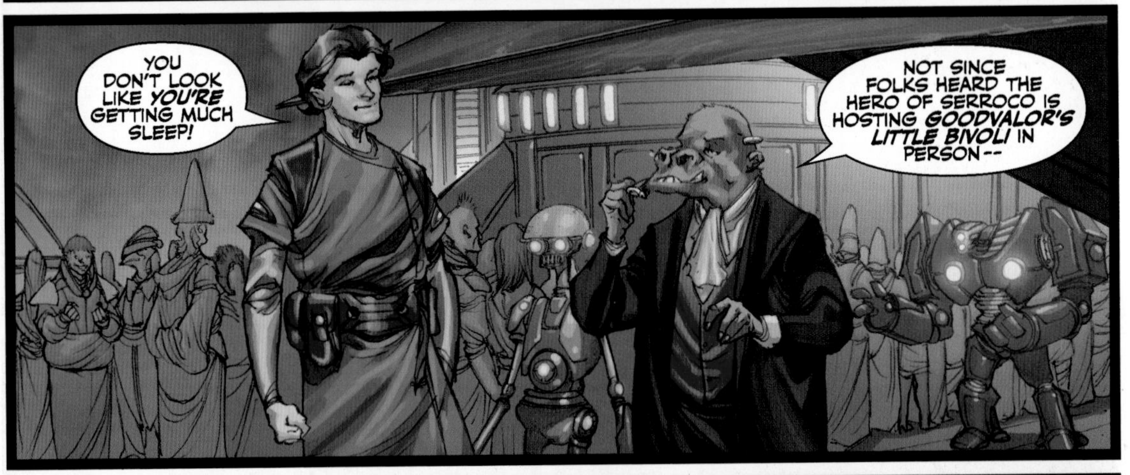
YOU DON'T LOOK LIKE *YOU'RE* GETTING MUCH SLEEP!
NOT SINCE FOLKS HEARD THE HERO OF SERROCO IS HOSTING ***GOODVALOR'S LITTLE BIVOLI*** IN PERSON --

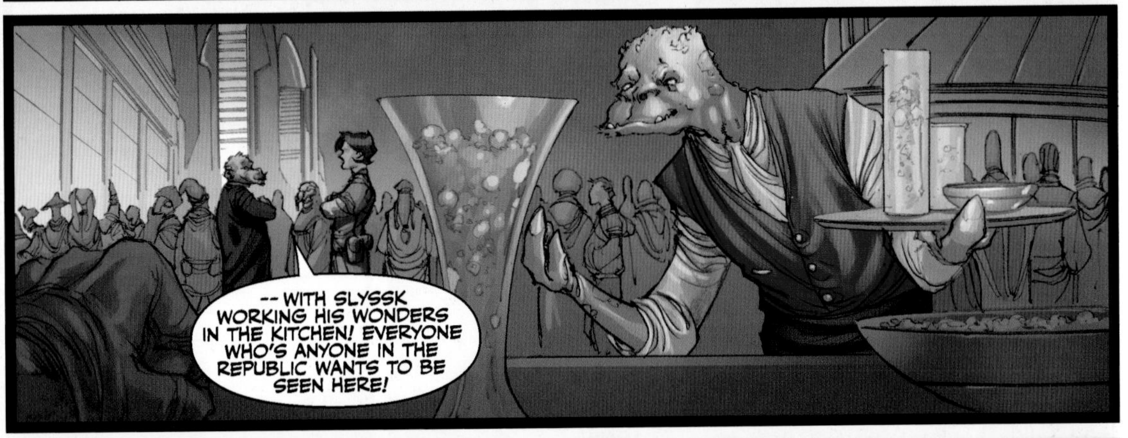
-- WITH SLYSSK WORKING HIS WONDERS IN THE KITCHEN! EVERYONE WHO'S ANYONE IN THE REPUBLIC WANTS TO BE SEEN HERE!

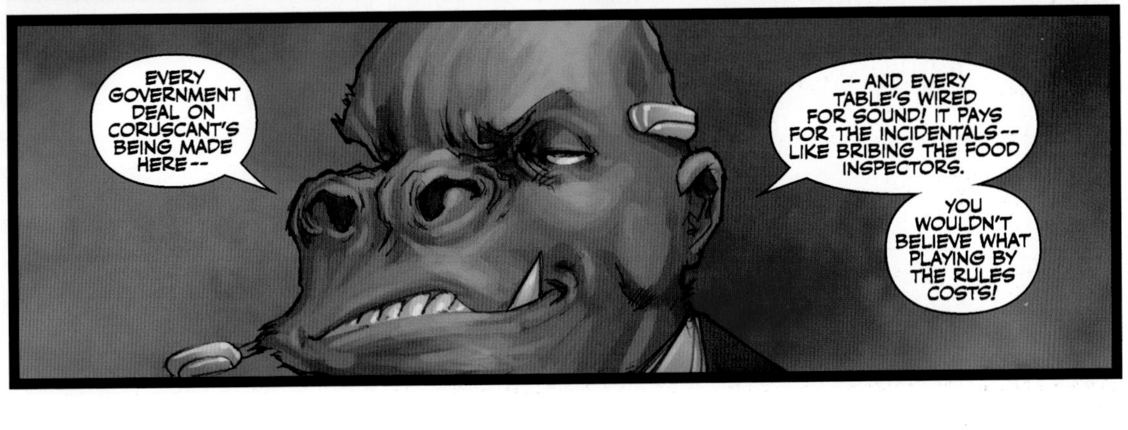
EVERY GOVERNMENT DEAL ON CORUSCANT'S BEING MADE HERE --
-- AND EVERY TABLE'S WIRED FOR SOUND! IT PAYS FOR THE INCIDENTALS -- LIKE BRIBING THE FOOD INSPECTORS.
YOU WOULDN'T BELIEVE WHAT PLAYING BY THE RULES COSTS!

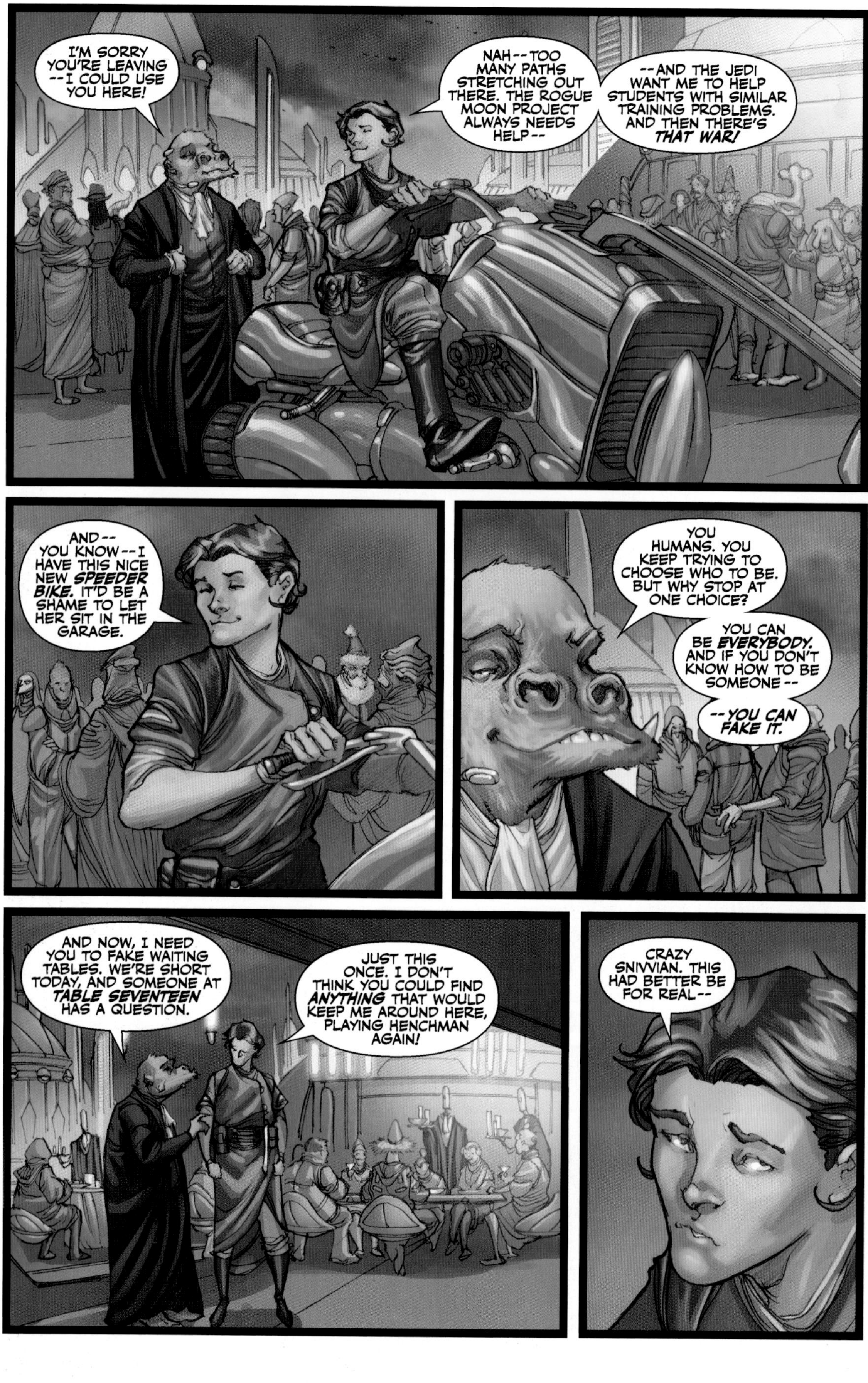
I'M SORRY YOU'RE LEAVING --I COULD USE YOU HERE!
NAH--TOO MANY PATHS STRETCHING OUT THERE. THE ROGUE MOON PROJECT ALWAYS NEEDS HELP--
--AND THE JEDI WANT ME TO HELP STUDENTS WITH SIMILAR TRAINING PROBLEMS. AND THEN THERE'S *THAT WAR!*
AND-- YOU KNOW--I HAVE THIS NICE NEW *SPEEDER BIKE.* IT'D BE A SHAME TO LET HER SIT IN THE GARAGE.
YOU HUMANS. YOU KEEP TRYING TO CHOOSE WHO TO BE. BUT WHY STOP AT ONE CHOICE?
YOU CAN BE *EVERYBODY.* AND IF YOU DON'T KNOW HOW TO BE SOMEONE--
--YOU CAN FAKE IT.
AND NOW, I NEED YOU TO FAKE WAITING TABLES. WE'RE SHORT TODAY, AND SOMEONE AT *TABLE SEVENTEEN* HAS A QUESTION.
JUST THIS ONCE. I DON'T THINK YOU COULD FIND *ANYTHING* THAT WOULD KEEP ME AROUND HERE, PLAYING HENCHMAN AGAIN!
CRAZY SNIVVIAN. THIS HAD BETTER BE FOR REAL--

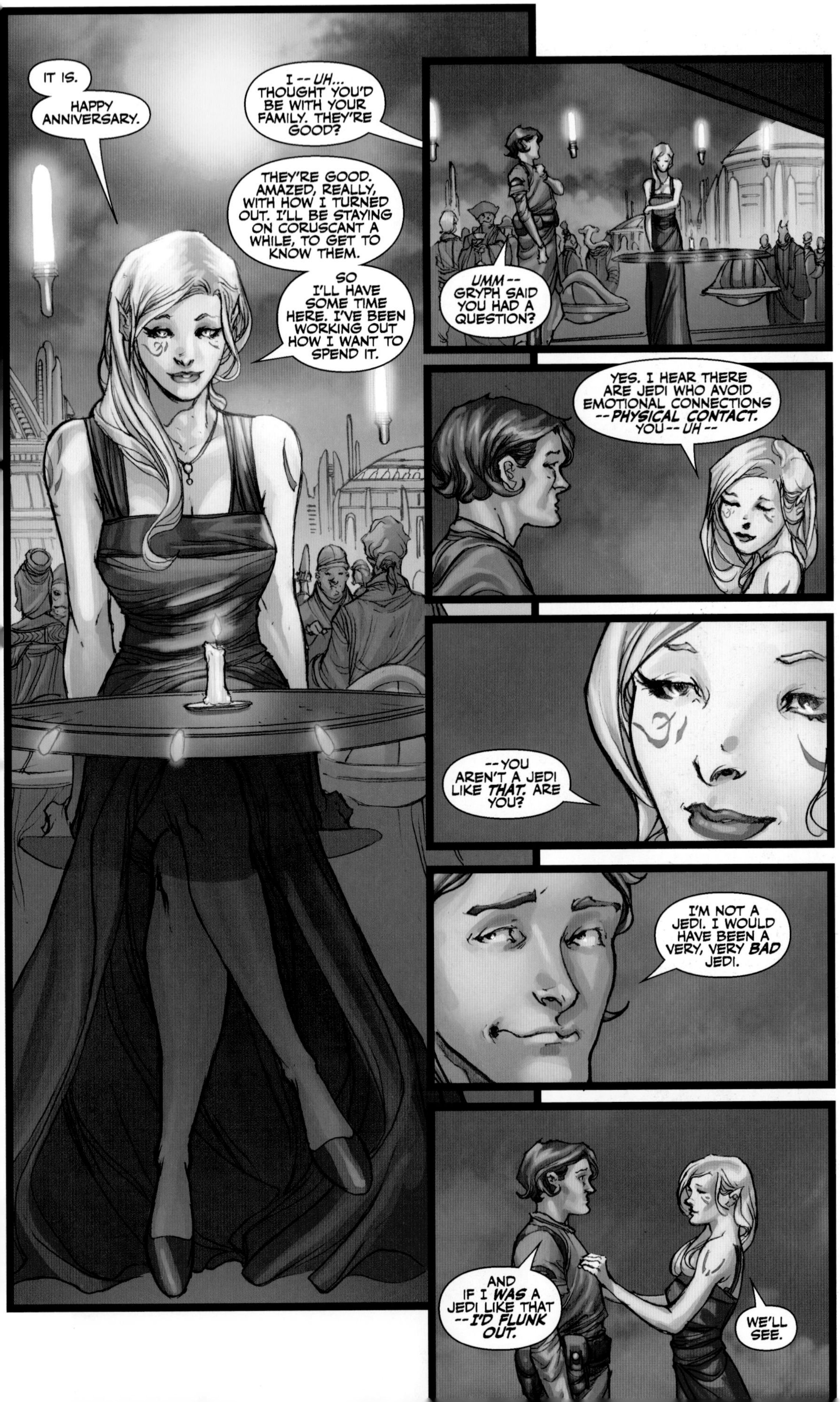
IT IS.
HAPPY ANNIVERSARY.
I -- UH... THOUGHT YOU'D BE WITH YOUR FAMILY. THEY'RE GOOD?
THEY'RE GOOD. AMAZED, REALLY, WITH HOW I TURNED OUT. I'LL BE STAYING ON CORUSCANT A WHILE, TO GET TO KNOW THEM.
SO I'LL HAVE SOME TIME HERE. I'VE BEEN WORKING OUT HOW I WANT TO SPEND IT.
UMM -- GRYPH SAID YOU HAD A QUESTION?
YES. I HEAR THERE ARE JEDI WHO AVOID EMOTIONAL CONNECTIONS --PHYSICAL CONTACT. YOU -- UH --
--YOU AREN'T A JEDI LIKE THAT, ARE YOU?
I'M NOT A JEDI. I WOULD HAVE BEEN A VERY, VERY BAD JEDI.
AND IF I WAS A JEDI LIKE THAT --I'D FLUNK OUT.
WE'LL SEE.

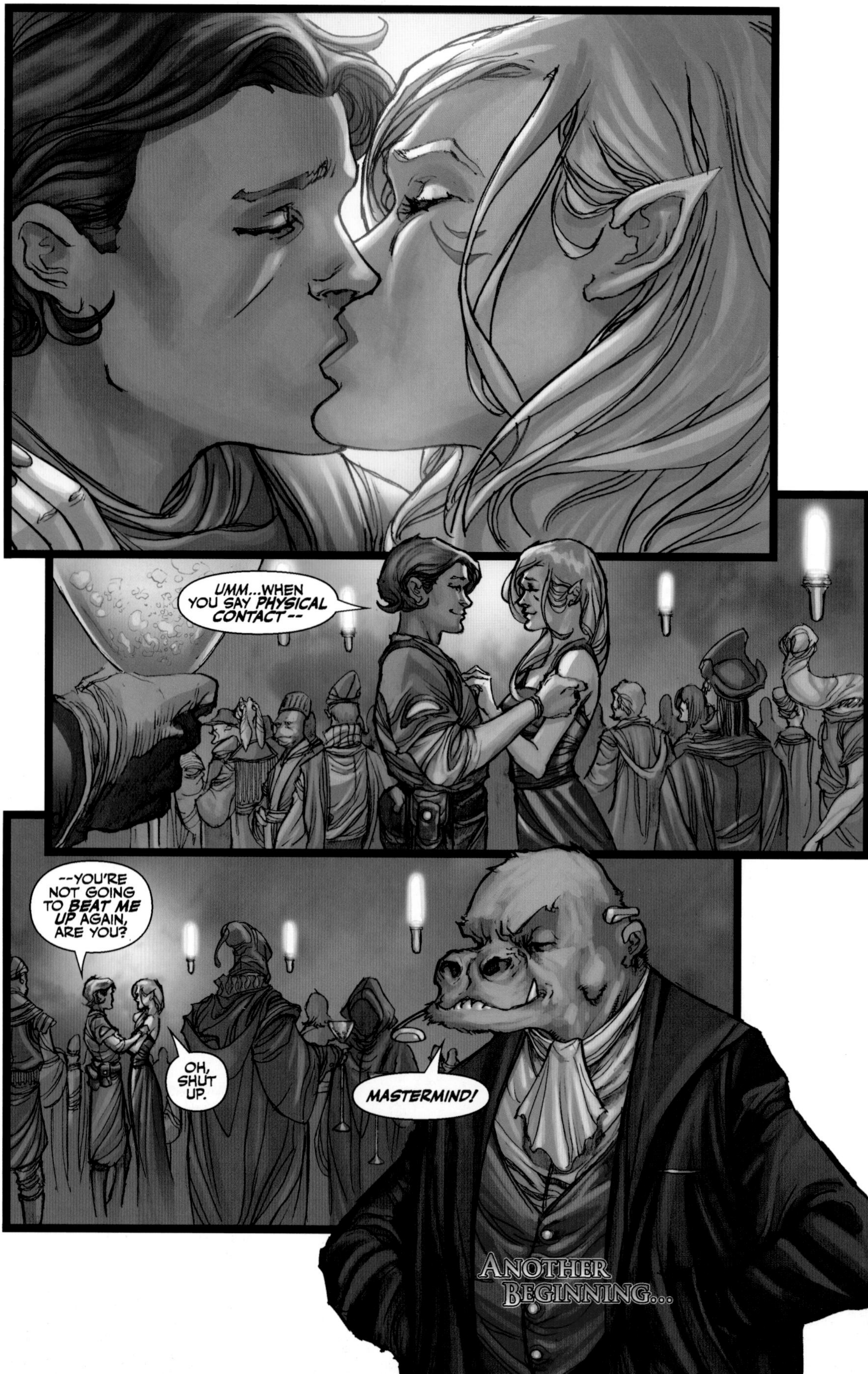
UMM...WHEN YOU SAY PHYSICAL CONTACT--
--YOU'RE NOT GOING TO BEAT ME UP AGAIN, ARE YOU?
OH, SHUT UP.
MASTERMIND!
ANOTHER BEGINNING...

STAR WARS®
KNIGHTS OF THE OLD REPUBLIC

TO FIND A COMICS SHOP IN YOUR AREA, CALL 1-888-266-4226.
For more information or to order direct: *On the web: darkhorse.com *E-mail: mailorder@darkhorse.com
*Phone: 1-800-862-0052 Mon.-Fri. 9 A.M. to 5 P.M. Pacific Time.

*prices and availability subject to change without notice. STAR WARS © 2010 Lucasfilm Ltd. & TM (BL 8023)

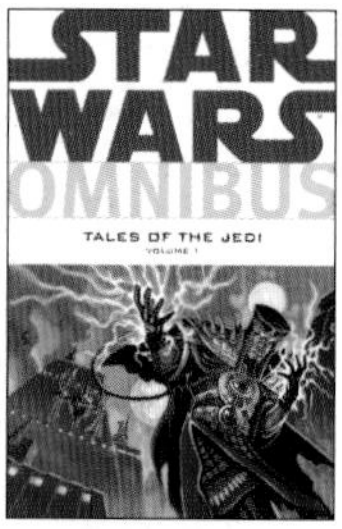
STAR WARS
OMNIBUS
TALES OF THE JEDI
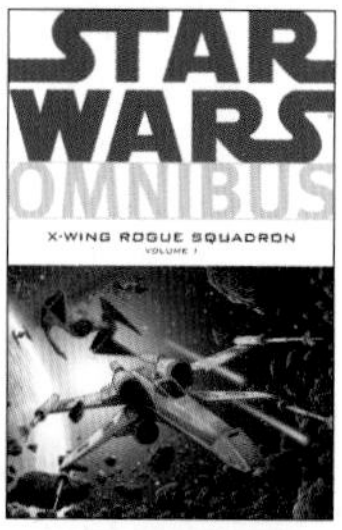
STAR WARS
OMNIBUS
X-WING ROGUE SQUADRON
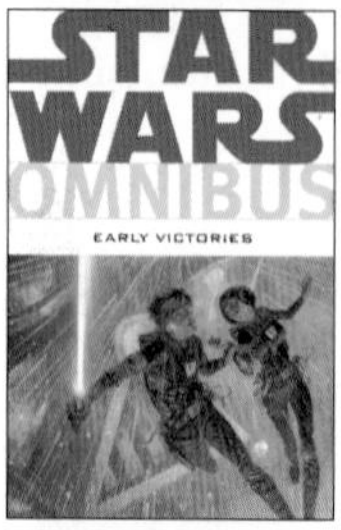
STAR WARS
OMNIBUS
EARLY VICTORIES
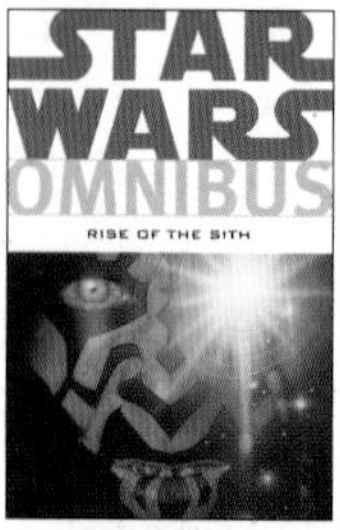
STAR WARS
OMNIBUS
RISE OF THE SITH
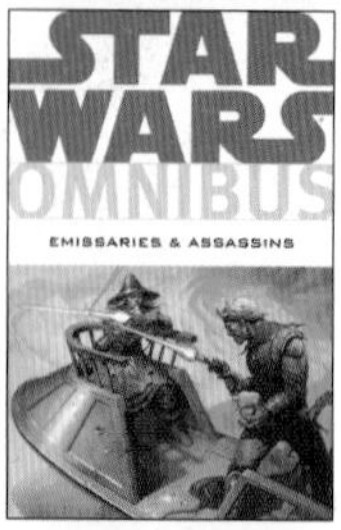
STAR WARS
OMNIBUS
EMISSARIES & ASSASSINS
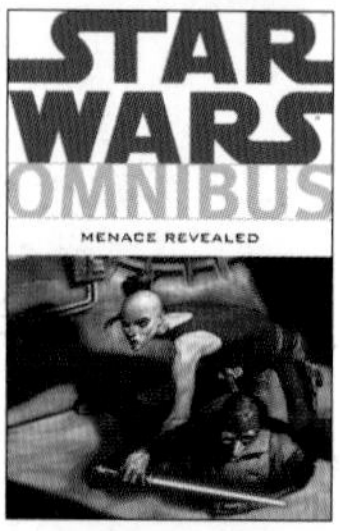
STAR WARS
OMNIBUS
MENACE REVEALED
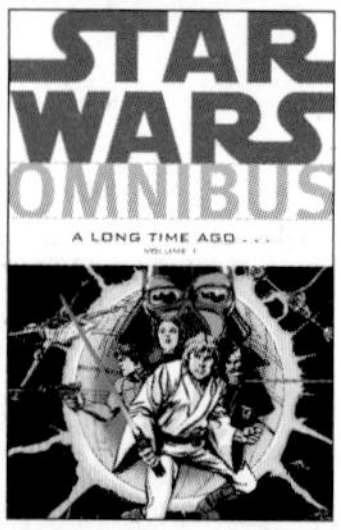
STAR WARS
OMNIBUS
A LONG TIME AGO . . .

STAR WARS OMNIBUS COLLECTIONS

STAR WARS: TALES OF THE JEDI

Including the *Tales of the Jedi* stories "The Golden Age of the Sith," "The Freedon Nadd Uprising," and "Knights of the Old Republic," these huge omnibus editions are the ultimate introduction to the ancient history of the *Star Wars* universe!

Volume 1 ISBN 978-1-59307-830-0 | $24.99 **Volume 2 ISBN 978-1-59307-911-6 | $24.99**

STAR WARS: X-WING ROGUE SQUADRON

The greatest starfighters of the Rebel Alliance become the defenders of a new Republic in this massive collection of stories featuring Wedge Antilles, hero of the Battle of Endor, and his team of ace pilots known throughout the galaxy as Rogue Squadron.

Volume 1 ISBN 978-1-59307-572-9 | $24.99 **Volume 2 ISBN 978-1-59307-619-1 | $24.99**
Volume 3 ISBN 978-1-59307-776-1 | $24.99

STAR WARS: BOBA FETT

Boba Fett, the most feared, most respected, and most loved bounty hunter in the galaxy, now has all of his comics stories collected into one massive volume!

ISBN 978-1-59582-418-9 | $24.99

STAR WARS: EARLY VICTORIES

Following the destruction of the first Death Star, Luke Skywalker is the new, unexpected hero of the Rebellion. But the galaxy hasn't been saved yet–Luke and Princess Leia find there are many more battles to be fought against the Empire and Darth Vader!

ISBN 978-1-59582-172-0 | $24.99

STAR WARS: RISE OF THE SITH

Before the name of Skywalker–or Vader–achieved fame across the galaxy, the Jedi Knights had long preserved peace and justice . . . as well as preventing the return of the Sith. These thrilling tales illustrate the events leading up to *The Phantom Menace*.

ISBN 978-1-59582-228-4 | $24.99

STAR WARS: EMISSARIES AND ASSASSINS

Discover more stories featuring Anakin Skywalker, Amidala, Obi-Wan, and Qui-Gon set during the time of Episode I: *The Phantom Menace* in this mega collection!

ISBN 978-1-59582-229-1 | $24.99

STAR WARS: MENACE REVEALED

This is our largest omnibus of never-before-collected and out-of-print *Star Wars* stories. Included here are one-shot adventures, short story arcs, specialty issues, and early Dark Horse Extra comic strips! All of these tales take place after Episode I: *The Phantom Menace*, and lead up to Episode II: *Attack of the Clones*.

ISBN 978-1-59582-273-4 | $24.99

STAR WARS: SHADOWS OF THE EMPIRE

Featuring all your favorite characters from the *Star Wars* trilogy—Luke Skywalker, Princess Leia, and Han Solo—this volume includes stories written by acclaimed novelists Timothy Zahn and Steve Perry!

ISBN 978-1-59582-434-9 | $24.99

STAR WARS: A LONG TIME AGO. . . .

Star Wars: A Long Time Ago. . . . omnibus volumes feature classic *Star Wars* stories not seen in over twenty years! Originally printed by Marvel Comics, these stories have been recolored and are sure to please *Star Wars* fans both new and old.

Volume 1: ISBN 978-1-59582-486-8 | $24.99 **Volume 2: ISBN 978-1-59582-554-4 | $24.99**

AVAILABLE AT YOUR LOCAL COMICS SHOP OR BOOKSTORE!
To find a comics shop in your area, call 1-888-266-4226
For more information or to order direct: • On the web: darkhorse.com
• E-mail: mailorder@darkhorse.com • Phone: 1-800-862-0052 Mon.–Fri. 9 AM to 5 PM Pacific Time